Death,
Judgment,
Heaven
& Hell

SAYINGS OF THE FATHERS OF THE CHURCH

Death,
Judgment,
Heaven
& Hell

Edited by Edward Condon

FOREWORD BY
C. C. PECKNOLD

 The Catholic University of America Press   Washington, D.C.

Copyright © 2019

The Catholic University of America Press

All rights reserved

The paper used in this publication meets the minimum requirements of American National Standards for Information Science—Permanence of Paper for Printed Library Materials, ANSI z39.48-1984.

∞

Cataloging-in-Publication Data available from the Library of Congress

ISBN 978-0-8132-3125-9

CONTENTS

FOREWORD BY C. C. PECKNOLD

In a loquacious age starved of truth, a single lapidary sentence of ancient wisdom can penetrate the mind and open it up to the first things as well as the last things. Ed Condon has given us a kind of cure by carefully arranging a patristic *florilegium* that draws from both East and West, Latin and Greek fathers alike. However beset we may feel by the daily consumption of a thousand banalities, we can now turn to this little work, which races ahead with the graces that flowed through the pens of these great early church fathers.

The fathers consistently show themselves to be masters of the sacred page. They hold together the old covenant with the new revealed in Christ. This is particularly evident when dealing with the four last things of death, judgment, heaven, and hell. Their thoroughly biblical understanding of the last things is all the more striking against a modern era that seems intent on denying all four of them.

As St. Peter Chrysologos notes, death itself will "run into its judge." Death, like birth, is the common lot of all of us. Try as we might, we can't dodge it. But as St. Hilary of Poitiers points out, "Death has its limits." For some, death is the just punishment for sin, but for others—as St. Augustine shows—death "secures for the soul a grace" that leads to eternal life. Unlike some modern theologians, the fathers all bear witness to an "intermediate state" between death and resurrection, and likewise each sees that all will rise in the flesh for judgment—according to either the virtue or the guilt in which we have a share. In this sense, the fathers would not say that death is the end. We will all survive the death of the body, but for some this will be endless death, while for others it will be the beginning of true life eternally. So death may be the first of last things, but it's not the end.

Just as all must die, so must all be judged. Justice itself must be brought to judgment. As Origen states, "All of us must appear before the judgment seat of Christ." So St. Gregory the Great points out, a thousand years before the development of the medieval doctrine of purgatory, that it is fitting for the faithful to endure "a cleansing fire before judgment, because of . . . Faults that remain to be purged away." Interestingly, the fathers teach that even this present life is a kind of purgation for some. Thus it behooves each of us to prepare for judgment and to constantly present ourselves, as St. Basil reminds us, before the judgment seat of Jesus Christ. Here there is hope even for St. Augustine's "Middling Christian," who is too sinful for sainthood, but too devoted not to win the friendship of the saints. God's justice is goodness, and it is inseparable from his mercy, which can never be unjust. The fire that purifies one will be the same fire that punishes another—so it is with justice and mercy.

Heaven is the greatest mercy and the supreme good to which we should order all lesser goods. For this reason we must understand heaven as both open and closed. The fathers are one with St. Jerome in finding heaven open to "the just and believers," just as it is closed to "sinners and unbelievers." But for all people there is a key. The key that unlocks heaven for all, as the martyrs show us, is in that Faith that unites our blood to Christ's blood. As St. John Chrysostom writes, "The Cross has taken away sin . . . it opened the gates of heaven." And so it is only through the gate of Christ's body, the church, that we may be rightly disposed to enter through the gate of Paradise.

Yet the key to heaven is not simply "faith alone" but the faith that works through charity and almsgiving. Each of the fathers identified "care of the poor" as a mark of those who will possess heaven. Similarly, Chrystostom warns that "no one will rescue you from hell except the assistance which you obtain from the poor."

While some modern theologians "dared to hope that all may be saved," for the vast majority of the early church fathers, hell cannot be empty any more than man can be denied free choice. As St. John the Damascene writes, "When God has done everything for a man's salvation, yet the man of his own accord remains obdurate and uncured," then there must be a place of eternal perdition for him just as there is for Judas. While the contrite hate sin more than they fear hell, as Augustine observed, the unrepentant hate hell but fail to fear sin—and there is a place for the unrepentant. The fathers have no doubt that hell is populated. What they "dare to hope" is that many may be saved by fleeing from sin into the merciful arms of the Father revealed to us in Jesus Christ by the power of the Holy Spirit.

Knowledge of these four last things plunge the believer into the substance of things hoped for—namely, God's everlasting mercy. As the Apostle Paul reminds us, "In hope we are saved" (Rom 8:24). Today we live in a world that suffers without hope. Some work to constantly distract us from the reality of the "last things." There is a denial of death even within the culture of death. There is the denial of the just judgment of God even within a world driven by the capricious judgments of the masses. There is a denial of hell even within a world that celebrates sin. Most tragic of all, we live in a world that finds it difficult to face present struggles precisely because it is starved of a trustworthy hope. As Pope Benedict XVI wrote in *Spe salvi,* "The present, even if it is arduous, can be lived and accepted if it leads towards a goal, if we can be sure of this goal, and if this goal is great enough to justify the effort of the journey" (1).

Rather than let us remain fixed on what is fleeting, Ed Condon carefully draws together the wisdom of these fathers to draw our gaze to the immovable things: death, judgment, heaven, and hell. I hope this marvelous book will draw readers not only into the contemplation of the four last things, but also to the wider and deeper study of the church fathers. Indeed, the sayings in this book are drawn from the Fathers of the Church series, which began many years ago in response to a request from Cardinal Gibbons of happy memory to provide fresh translations of patristic materials that were suitable for a Catholic audience.

Here, in these pages, you will find truths that crush error, illumine darkness, and plunge us ever deeper into the truth of God's mercy. I warmly commend these pages to you as patristic lights to illumine our pilgrimage through this vale of tears to the City of God, for the good of all souls, across the centuries.

EDITOR'S NOTE

In the Venerable Bede's *Ecclesiastical History of the English People*, he recounts a pagan nobleman advising his king on the arrival of two Catholic missionaries. Consider, he suggests to the king, that this great hall is the world. A bird flies in from the storm, circles this fire two or three times, and departs again into the dark. We are this bird, he observes; we know not where we came from, or where we are going. He concludes that if these men can tell them something of this mystery, they should be made welcome.

Man's confrontation with death, and how he should live his life illuminated by this inevitability, is the deepest concern of the human condition. It has preoccupied the greatest philosophers of human history. The wisdom of the church addressing the eschatological realties of the four last things—death, judgment, heaven, and hell—is profound indeed. Pope Benedict XVI, while still Cardinal Ratzinger, wrote *Eschatology: Death and Eternal Life* (published by The Catholic University of America Press), and great minds like his can offer a rich understanding of the metaphysics of the hereafter. But in the simple language of the Penny Catechism, we are reminded that to love and serve God in this life is our sacred purpose on earth, one that looks forward to our eternal purpose— to be happy with him forever in the next.

As we, as Christians, pick our way through daily life, the words of the saints concerning our proper destination can be a surprisingly direct light for our path. The quotes selected for this slim volume remind us of the real promise of heaven that we have all received, and urge us to prepare for our inevitable meeting with our Creator. They provide the, at times blunt, reminder that while the mercy of God and the blessings of heaven are held out to us, in the end we choose, through our daily actions, our road to heaven or to hell.

So far as possible, the quotations have been arranged for readability so that the Fathers of the Church can be found almost in dialogue with each other, and with us. While casual, even random reading can admonish and edify the reader in equal measure, it is to be hoped that it can also inspire readers to return to the original sources and hear the fathers in full.

The Church has traditionally always spoken of the four last things in this order: death, judgement, heaven, and hell. In their own treatments of the four last things, some of the fathers consciously broke with this order, choosing to end with heaven, rather than hell. Yet in reading them together, the sense grows that the damned are those who remain outside, left behind, truly the last. For this reason, the traditional order has been preserved here.

Considering our death and judgment is the work of a whole life. The fathers sought more often to caution and inspire than to console and sooth when speaking of heaven and hell. In the end, as we know from the Didache, the earliest of Christian catecheses, "There are two ways, one of life and one of death; and great is the difference between the two ways."

It is for each of us on earth to choose our way.

Death,
Judgment,
Heaven
& Hell

Death

Beginning

1 This, then, is the function of death—the complete separation of body and soul. **Tertullian, *On the Soul*, 52.1**

2 In the Scriptures, "death" is a single term, but signifies many things. For the separation of the body from the soul is called death. But this cannot be said to be either good or bad; it is neutral. **Origen, *Commentary on the Epistle to the Romans*, 6.6.5**

3 Men have distinguished two forms of death—the ordinary and the extraordinary. An ordinary death is a calm and peaceful end and it is ascribed to nature; any violent death is considered extraordinary and contrary to nature. **Tertullian, *On the Soul*, 52.1**

4 Just as the soul dies when God abandons it, so too the body dies when the soul abandons it, whence the former becomes foolish and the latter becomes lifeless. **St. Augustine, *The Trinity*, 4.3.5**

5 There are many kinds of death: some taste death; others see death; still others eat it; some are glutted by it; others again are renewed by it. **St. Jerome, *Homilies*, 80**

The Origin of Death

6 God, who has the power to raise the dead, is the One who permitted us to die. He who can restore life is the One who permitted men to be killed. **St. Peter Chrysologos, *Sermons*, 1.101**

7 Sin is the father of death. If there had been no sin, there would have been no death. **St. Augustine, *Sermons of the Liturgical Seasons*, 231.2**

8 Yet death is imposed on the body because of sin, that is to say that it might not sin. **Origen, *Commentary on the Epistle to the Romans*, 6.13.5**

9 Death, which is inflicted as the penalty of sin, is a purification on the sin itself for which it was ordered to be inflicted. **Origen, *Homilies on Leviticus*, 14.4.2**

10 From where, then, did death come? By the envy of the Devil death came into the world. **Origen, *Homilies on Jeremiah*, 2.1**

11 We know that death results from sin, and that neither death nor sin is a natural result of man's nature. **Tertullian, *On the Soul*, 52.2**

12 Death itself [is] the result of man's voluntary choice. Had he not sinned, he would not have died. **Tertullian, *On the Soul*, 52.2**

13 The way of death for us was through the sin of Adam. The devil is the mediator of this way, the one who persuades us to sin and hurled us headlong into death. **St. Augustine, *The Trinity*, 4.12.15**

14 God inflicted death, not as its first author, but as the avenger of sin. **St. Augustine, *Against Julian*, 9.36**

15 Death, in fact, was not in nature, but it became a part of nature. God did not establish death in the beginning but gave it as a remedy. **St. Ambrose, *On His Brother Satyrus*, 2.47**

16 Nor did God create death; man, in a way, is the founder and creator of evil. **St. Gregory of Nyssa, *On Virginity*, 12**

17 When death came as a necessary consequence for the human transgressions, human life was divided into two parts. One part is spent in the flesh, the other part after this is spent outside the body. **St. Gregory of Nyssa, *On the Soul and the Resurrection (Ascetical Works*, 233)**

18 Man, formed by the holy skill of God, whom the serpent deceived by his guile, took up death for himself beyond what was fated and chose knowledge of good and evil. **Lactantius, *The Divine Institutes*, 2.12**

Christ Conquered Death

19 Heavens, how great is the strength of Him who was crucified! He has persuaded men, who are to die and perish, that death is not death. **St. John Chrysostom, *Commentary on St. John the Apostle and Evangelist*, 2.444**

20 Believe in Christ made mortal for you, that you may grasp him immortal; for when you grasp his immortality, neither will you be mortal. God conquered death, that death might not conquer man. **St. Augustine, *Tractates on John*, 14.13.3**

21 We abused our immortality, and so died; Christ used his mortality well, and so we live. **St. Augustine, *On Christian Teaching*, 1.14.13**

22 When you grasp His immortality, neither will you be mortal. God conquered death, that death might not conquer man. **St. Augustine, *Tractates on John*, 14.13.3**

23 O death, when you embraced my Lord, then you died so far as I am concerned. **St. Augustine, *Sermons of the Liturgical Seasons*, 233.4**

24 Do not fear death any longer; what you feared has been conquered by the Lord. **St. Augustine, *Sermons of the Liturgical Seasons*, 253.2**

25 Death gets judged—death which, rushing against guilty men, runs into its Judge; death which, after long domination over its slaves, rose against its Master; death, which waxed fierce against men but encountered God. **St. Peter Chrysologos, *Sermons*, 1.74**

26 [In the Gospel] the order of things is changed. Here the sepulcher swallows death, not a dead man. The abode of death becomes a life-giving dwelling. A new kind of womb conceives one who is dead and brings him forth alive. **St. Peter Chrysologos, *Sermons*, 1.74**

27 Death is destroyed and completely swallowed up, now that life has arisen. **St. Caesarius of Arles, *Sermons*, 69.2**

28 No sooner had the devil's malice put us to death with the poison of envy than the almighty and merciful God immediately foreshadowed the remedy of his care. **St. Leo the Great, *Sermons*, 22.1.2**

29 Purged of the ancient contagion [of the devil], nature returns to its dignity, death is dispelled by [Christ's] death, birth restored by [His] birth. **St. Leo the Great, *Sermons*, 22.4.2**

30 Unless Almighty God were willing [to be born of Mary], no superficial justice, no sketchy wisdom could rescue anyone from the devil's captivity and the abyss of eternal death. **St. Leo the Great, *Sermons*, 24.2.1**

31 Almighty God, therefore, made our extremely bad situation good through his unique lowliness and destroyed death along with the author of death. **St. Leo the Great, *Sermons*, 37.3**

32 The universal edict of death which proclaimed our sale into bondage has been made void, and the contractual rights have been transferred to the Redeemer. **St. Leo the Great, *Sermons*, 61.4**

33 He endured previous sorrows even to the point of death. No one could be released from the fetters of mortality unless He, in whom alone the nature of all people was innocent, should allow Himself to be killed by the hands of wicked men. **St. Leo the Great, *Sermons*, 63.4**

34 When this fear residing in the flesh was cast out, when the flesh then made the transition over to the Father's will, and when the whole threat of death was trampled underfoot, He was fulfilling the work of His design. **St. Leo the Great, *Sermons*, 67.7**

35 First Adam and Second Adam were one with respect to human flesh but not when it came to their respective work. In the former "all die." In the latter "all will be brought to life." **St. Leo the Great, *Sermons*, 69.3.2**

36 Since death is nothing other than the dissolution of body and soul, he who unites himself to both, that is, to both body and soul, is separated from neither of them. But having given a share of himself to both body and soul, Christ opened paradise for the thief through the soul, while through the body he put a stop to the power of decay. **St. Gregory of Nyssa, *Refutation of the Views of Apolinarius*, 11**

37 Thus, by the ineffable mercy of God, the penalty of sin is transformed into the panoply of virtue and the punishment of the sinner into the testing of the saint. **St. Augustine, *City of God*, 13.4**

38 No one is immortal, since no one is of heaven. And so, to undo the chain of this sin and death, the Almighty Son of God, filling all things, containing all things, equal in all things to the Father, and coeternal in one essence (from Him and with Him), took on Himself our human nature. **St. Leo the Great, *Sermons*, 24.2.2**

All Men Must Die

39 Absolutely every man who is born must also, by reason of a debt, be subject to death. Thus when we liquidate this debt, we render thanks. **St. Justin Martyr, *Second Apology*, 11**

40 You were born a man, and therefore mortal; why, then, do you repine because something has happened in accordance with nature? **St. John Chrysostom, *Commentary on St. John the Apostle and Evangelist*, 2.178**

41 This life of ours ... bears witness to the fact that, from its very start, the race of mortal men has been a race condemned. **St. Augustine, *City of God*, 22.22**

42 Man longs to live, but is forced to die; but how can any man be said to live as he longs to live who does not live as long as he longs to live? **St. Augustine, *City of God*, 14.25**

43 This is indeed a dying life, whatever mortal comfort it may shower on us, whatever companions my share it with us, whatever wealth of worldly goods it may lavish on us. **St. Augustine, *Letters*, 130, p. 381**

44 What harm is it for beings destined to die to lose the life of the flesh? And what do those who fear death achieve except to die a little later? **St. Augustine, *Letters*, 151, p. 274**

45 Therefore, every man is born subject to this condition of death, subject to these laws of the lower world, with the sole exception of that Man who became Man so that man might not perish. **St. Augustine, *Sermons of the Liturgical Seasons*, 231.2**

46 The earth is full of these two wares: birth and death. **St. Augustine, *Sermons of the Liturgical Seasons*, 233.3**

47 No man is believed to acquire immortality unless he first tastes death. **St. Augustine, *Eight Questions of Dulcitius*, Question 3**

48 The fact is that only a living man can be said to be dying. **St. Augustine, *City of God*, 13.9**

49 The course of life is nothing but a race towards death, a race in which one may stand still or slow down even for a moment, but all must run with equal speed and never changing stride. For, to the short-lived as to the long-lived, each day passes with unchanging pace. **St. Augustine, *City of God*, 13.10**

50 Death will come to all men, but not in every case will it be a death for Christ. **St. Augustine, *Selected Sermons*, 5.1 (Den)**

51 He is a fool who thinks he can conquer death, since he cannot know death or its substance. **St. Ephrem the Syrian, *The Hymns on Faith*, 11.15**

52 Consider: even if we do not die right now, shall we not eventually? Shall we not keep faith with our mortality? Let us turn necessity into glorious opportunity; let us give meaning to our death; let us make what is common to all something specially ours; let us purchase life with death. **St. Gregory of Nazianzus, *Selected Orations*, 15.7**

53 It is a great mystery of divine love that not even Christ was exempted from bodily death and that, even though Lord of nature, He did not object to the law of the flesh which He had taken upon Himself. I must die. **St. Ambrose, *On His Brother Satyrus*, 1.4**

54 To die is a matter of nature; it is necessary to perish. Our ancestors lived for us; we live for future men; no one lives for himself. It is part of virtue to will what cannot be avoided. Willingly accept that to which you are being pressed with reluctance. **St. Peter Chrysologos, *Sermons*, 1.101**

55 Since there is nothing that can ward off the inevitable torture of this evil, it is necessary to tolerate what no man can escape. **Braulio of Saragossa, *Letters*, 29**

56 It troubles some that we have this mortality in common with others. But what in this world do we not have in common with others as long as this flesh, in accord with the law of our original birth, still remains common to us? **St. Cyprian, *Mortality*, 8**

Fear of Death

57 So great is the love of this life that even when just cause for death is at hand, hardly anyone receives death patiently. **Origen, *Commentary on the Epistle to the Romans*, 4.11.1**

58 Inordinate grief, or dread of death, is not a minor evil. How many has it driven to suicide by rope or blade! **St. Ambrose, *On His Brother Satyrus*, 2.11**

59 Do not let this separation from the world trouble you. For, if we reflect that it is the very world that is more truly a prison, we shall realize that you have left a prison, rather than entered one. **Tertullian, *To the Martyrs*, 2.1**

60 Death is not feared but hoped for, which, indeed, is conquered but the reward of immortality. **St. Cyprian, *Letters*, 37.3**

61 If we could escape death, we might justly fear to die. But since it is necessary for the mortal to die, let us embrace the opportunity coming from the divine promise ... let us go through the exit of death with the reward of immortality. **St Cyprian, *Letters*, 58.2**

62 We struggle in opposition and resist and in the manner of obstinate slaves we are brought with sadness and grief to the sight of God, departing from here under the bond of necessity. **St. Cyprian, Mortality, 18**

63 Death is not to be feared, nor need we anticipate any end of those blessings [which come from Christ]. **St. John Chrysostom, Commentary on St. John the Apostle and Evangelist, 1.401**

64 Death is an awesome thing, and one that inspires great fear—not, however, to those who have knowledge of the true wisdom from above. **St. John Chrysostom, Commentary on St. John the Apostle and Evangelist, 2.399**

65 The man who has no clear understanding of the life to come, but considers death as a kind of annihilation and end of life, with good reason shudders and is afraid. **St. John Chrysostom, Commentary on St. John the Apostle and Evangelist, 2.399**

66 Let us not, then, tremble at the thought of death. Naturally, our soul has a strong desire for life, but there lies within us the power to free it from these bonds. **St. John Chrysostom, Commentary on St. John the Apostle and Evangelist, 2.432**

67 The philosophers say—rightly say—that the first and most fundamental command of nature is that a man should cherish his own human life, and, by his very nature, shun death; a man should be his own best friend. **St. Augustine, City of God, 19.4**

68 Understand this now: when you feared to die, then you died. For he, Peter, died by denying; but he rose with his weeping. **St. Augustine, Sermons of the Liturgical Seasons, 253.2**

69 Those who are faithful neither fear nor tremble at their dissolution, but desire and long for it to come, because they realize that through death peace, and not punishment, is offered to them. **St. Augustine, *The Christian Life*, 5**

70 To be reluctant to die is typical of human fear; to have arisen from death is a mark of divine power. **St. Peter Chrysologos, *Sermons*, 1.61**

71 Why do you consider your life here as something great and these few days as many, and turn from this separation, which is welcome and sweet as if it were something previous and horrible? **St. Gregory of Nazianzus, *On His Brother St. Caesarius*, 22**

72 Not wishing to die is characteristic of human fear; dying and rising characterize God alone. **St. Peter Chrysologos, *Sermons*, 3.72.4**

73 It is a characteristic of a shameless debtor either to postpone what is due or to deny what he has promised; an honorable one, by contrast, makes good on both pledges without delay and readily. **St. Peter Chrysologos, *Sermons*, 3.123.1**

74 You are a fish caught in the net of the Church. Let yourself be taken alive: don't try to escape. It is Jesus who is playing you on His line, not to kill you, but, by killing you, to make you alive. For you must die and rise again. **St. Cyril of Jerusalem, *Procatechesis*, 5**

75 If you are not afraid to be cattle [in your senseless way of living], at least fear to die like them. **St. Caesarius of Arles, *Sermons*, 100.6**

76 The source of great fear, if one is not forgiven of his sins by Christ, is the dissolution of death, because no one who has not been pardoned from sin may return to his eternal home. **St. Hilary of Poitiers, *Commentary on Matthew*, 8.8**

77 Let no one "fear to suffer for justice," or be anxious about the repayment of the promises, because we pass through labor to rest, and through death to life. **St. Leo the Great, *Sermons*, 51.8**

78 For the continuous expectation of death is not known through spoken symbols, but because of the uncertainty of the future, inherently frightening, it dissipates our present joy and disturbs our well-being with the fear of what is to come. **St. Gregory of Nyssa, *On Virginity*, 3**

79 We see every human effort directed towards this, namely, how to remain alive.... Isn't concern for life altogether due to the fear of death? **St. Gregory of Nyssa, *On the Soul and the Resurrection* (*Ascetical Works*, p. 199)**

80 With all the risks that threaten daily life, every mortal is exposed to every kind of death and is uncertain which of them he will meet, I ask which is preferable: to suffer one death once for all, or to keep on living in constant dread of them all? **St. Augustine, *City of God*, 1.11**

Preparing for Death

81 Who is the one who dies in peace if not he who has the peace of God, which surpasses every perception and guards the heart of him who possesses it? **Origen, *Homilies on Luke*, 15.4**

82 Let no one think of death, but of immortality, nor of punishment in time, but of glory everlasting. **St. Cyprian, *Letters*, 6.2**

83 You are planning for a long life; do you not fear a sudden death? **St. Augustine, *Sermons of the Liturgical Seasons*, 232.7**

84 For this reason, I beg the privilege of enjoying the cure in this present life, since I know that no cure will then be granted those departing this life with wounds, as there is no longer any room for repentance. **Theodoret of Cyrus, *Commentary on the Psalms*, 6.5**

85 Let us not say to one another: "Let us eat and drink for tomorrow we shall die." But for the very reason that the day of death is uncertain and the day of life is troublesome, let us fast and pray more earnestly "for tomorrow we shall die." **St. Augustine, *Sermons of the Liturgical Seasons*, 210.5**

86 In any hour, you may perish; look out, lest while you are intending to bury the dead, you die yourself. **St. Jerome, *Homilies*, 85**

87 Bear up, O just ones, endure for a while. Yea, more, even grant a truce to your opponents. This short-lived mingling with the unjust will be compensated by a long separation. **St. Peter Chrysologos, *Sermons*, 1.47**

88 Fruitful and happy the mind and heart that day and night are filled with longing for the dwelling pace of the Lord! When death comes to the sinner, his thought is not on that dwelling place, but on punishments; he does not meditate upon the kingdom of Heaven, but is in dread of the flames of hell. **St. Jerome, *Homilies*, 63**

89 To the first death, which is the separation of the soul from the body, all alike, both righteous and sinners, are subject, so that the divine pronouncement may achieve its end: "You are dust and to dust you shall return." But the second death, of sin, which the Lord mentions when he says "Leave the dead to bury their dead," would not injure those who conquer their temptations. **Oecumenius, *Commentary on the Apocalypse*, 2.5**

90 An old man said: "A man who has death before his eyes at every hour conquers meanness of spirit." **Martin of Braga, *Sayings of the Egyptian Fathers*, 95**

91 Think of people who happen to be living in a foreign land: when they have in mind to return home, for a long time beforehand they begin to develop an enthusiasm and take pains to collect enough provisions to enable them to last the length of the journey.... It should be exactly like this in our case. **St. John Chrysostom, *Homilies on Genesis*, 5.3**

92 You keep on adding to tomorrow and another tomorrow but neglect to be converted, and do you not fear that sudden death may overtake you? **St. Caesarius of Arles, *Sermons*, 18.1**

93 If God wanted you to perish, He would have taken you away when you were sinning. Since you have sinned so much and still live, you are invited to repentance. **St. Caesarius of Arles, *Sermons*, 18.4**

94 What is the health of body which death destroys and sickness weakens? It is worthless, mortal, and uncertain. Seek God, search for Him and do so freely; seek Him for His own sake, not yours. **St. Caesarius of Arles, *Sermons*, 137.2**

95 If, then, death is not able to outwit virginity, but through it comes to an end and ceases to be, this is clear proof that virginity is stronger than death. **St. Gregory of Nyssa, *On Virginity*, 14**

Dying

96 Though death [may] come in various ways (and there are many), no death is so easy as not to be in some sense violent. **Tertullian, *On the Soul*, 52.3**

97 When death comes suddenly, as from decapitation, it opens at once a large outlet for the soul. **Tertullian, *On the Soul*, 53.4**

98 Yet death is always much too violent, coming as it does by means alien to man's nature, in its own time, and snatching man from life just when he could pass his days in joy, happiness, honor, peace, and pleasure. **Tertullian, *On the Soul*, 52.3**

99 What difference does it make what kind of death puts an end to life, when one from whom it is taken away is not obliged to die again? **St. Augustine, *City of God*, 1.11**

100   It makes no difference if the ship of life goes to the bottom with its timbers intact, or shattered by a gale, so long as its power of navigation is destroyed.   **Tertullian, *On the Soul*, 52.4**

101   Whatever misfortune befalls the dying comes from their life, not their death.   **St. Augustine, *Letters*, 151, p. 274**

102   If you cling to the earth when heaven lies before you, consider how great an insult this is to the Giver.   **St. John Chrysostom, *Commentary on St. John the Apostle and Evangelist*, 1.311**

103   Who is the one who dies in peace if not he who has the peace of God, which surpasses every perception and guards the heart of him who possesses it?   **Origen, *Homilies on Luke*, 15.4**

104   Who is the one who departs in peace from this world if not he who understands that God was in Christ, reconciling the world to Himself?   **Origen, *Homilies on Luke*, 15.4**

105   No death is to be deemed evil which has been preceded by a good life; nor can anything make death evil save what follows it.   **St. Augustine, *City of God*, 1.11**

106   It is difficult, then, for anyone to live and not see death. [Yet] there is a difference between seeing death and tasting death. He who sees, sees assuredly, but does not taste; he who tastes, however, must necessarily see.   **St. Jerome, *Homilies*, 80**

107   And this alone is your gain from life here, to be brought through the confusion of things which are seen and unstable to things which are firm and immovable.   **St. Gregory of Nazianzus, *On His Brother St. Caesarius*, 19**

108   It sometimes happens that the soul in the moment of its departure … will show a piercing gaze, and talk a great deal … it enunciates, by means of its last remnant clinging to the flesh, the things which it sees and hears and is now beginning to know. **Tertullian, *On the Soul*, 53.5**

109 We should also know that frequently the sound of heavenly singing accompanies the death of the elect, and, while they listen to it with great delight, they are preserved from feeling pain at the separation of the soul and body. **St. Gregory the Great, *Dialogues*, 4.15**

110 It sometimes happens that the soul in the moment of its departure … will show a piercing gaze, and talk a great deal … it enunciates, by means of its last remnant clinging to the flesh, the things which it sees and hears and is now beginning to know. **Tertullian, *On the Soul*, 53.5**

111 It frequently happens that a soul on the point of death recognizes those with whom it is to share the same eternal dwelling for equal blame or reward. **St. Gregory the Great, *Dialogues*, 4.36.**

112 In His unbounded mercy, the good Lord allows some souls to return to their bodies shortly after death, so that the sight of hell might at last teach them to fear the eternal punishments in which words alone could not make them believe. **St. Gregory the Great, *Dialogues*, 4.37**

113 Whenever the enemy tempts your mind with fear or greed or anger, answer him boldly with words: "I have renounced and shall continue to renounce you and your work and your emissaries, because I believe in the living God and in his Son and Spirit and, stamped as I am, I no longer fear death." **Niceta of Remesiana, *Explanation of the Creed*, 14**

114 I ask what is preferable: to suffer one form of death once for all, or to keep on living in constant dread of all? **St. Augustine, *City of God*, 1.11**

115 If the choice had to be made between this and death, who would not choose to die? **St. Augustine, *City of God*, 21.14**

Martyrdom

116 Life is not taken away from Christians, but is changed for the better. **Braulio of Saragossa, *Letters*, 34**

117 The martyrs seek to save their souls. They lose their lives to save their souls. **Origen, *Homilies on Luke*, 36.1**

118 For a death which is sustained on account of piety and truth is precious in your sight. **Origen, *Commentary on the Epistle to the Romans*, 2.14.19**

119 Here, then, is the difference between pagan and Christian in death: If you lay down your life for God as the Paraclete recommends, then this will not be of some gentle fever in a soft bed, but in the torture of martyrdom. **Tertullian, *On the Soul*, 55.5**

120 To be sure, many Christians perished—some of them by the foulest kinds of death. If this is to be lamented, we nevertheless must recall that death is the common lot of all who have been born on earth. **St. Augustine, *City of God*, 1.11**

121 When a man dies out of faith and loyalty to the truth, he escapes death. **St. Augustine, *City of God*, 13.8**

122 Dearest children, in my eyes you are not dead but vowed in full flower to God; have not vanished, but changed abode; not been torn apart but been joined firmly together. **St. Gregory of Nazianzus, *Selected Orations*, 15.9**

123 But because we do not place our hope in the present, we do not mind when men murder us, since death is inevitable anyhow. **St. Justin Martyr, *First Apology*, 11**

124 Christ, in an address worthy of a king, urges His soldiers to despise death and to have no fear of those who kill the body. **St. Peter Chrysologos, *Sermons*, 1.101**

125 [Nero] seemed to think that the grace of God might be cut off by the slaughter of His holy ones. He did not know that the religion founded on the mystery of the Cross cannot be extinguished by any kind of cruelty, since "precious in the eyes of the Lord is the death of His holy ones." This does not diminish, but it increases, the Church. **St. Leo the Great, *Sermons*, 82.6**

126 The Lord wishes us to rejoice and to exult in persecutions since, when persecutions are carried on ... then the heavens lie open to the martyrs. **St. Cyprian, *Letters*, 58.2**

127 As the Lord tasted death in his circumstances, he showed the faithful how the drink of death has its limits. And so his words are followed by deeds. **St. Hilary of Poitiers, *Commentary on Matthew*, 17.1**

128 The souls of the faithfully departed think lightly of the death which has separated them from their bodies, because their flesh is now resting in hope, whatever abuse it may have seemed to suffer once all feeling was gone. **St. Augustine, *City of God*, 13.20**

129 Although death is the punishment of sin, sometimes it secures for the soul a grace that is security against all punishment for sin. **St. Augustine, *City of God*, 13.6**

130 Therefore, sin is absolved through the penalty of death and nothing remains which the day of judgment and the penalty of eternal fire will find for this offense. **Origen, *Homilies on Leviticus*, 14.4.2**

131 [The Evangelist] says, "Do not fear the tribulation from the enemies of God through afflictions and trials, for it will only last ten days and not be long lived." For this reason, death must be despised, since in a little while it grants "the unfading crown of life." **Andrew of Caesarea, Commentary on the Apocalypse, 2.10**

The Faithful Departed

132 For the death of the saints is rather sleep than death, since "they have labored unto eternity and shall live unto the end," and "precious in the eyes of the Lord is the death of his saints." **St. John of Damascus, Orthodox Faith, 4.15**

133 These [saints] of whom we speak are not dead. Because Life itself and the Author of life was reckoned amongst the dead, we do not call these dead who have fallen asleep in the hope of resurrection and in the faith in Him. For how could a dead body work miracles [like the relics of the saints]? **St. John of Damascus, Orthodox Faith, 4.15**

134 Does the thought of separation grieve you? Then let hope cheer you. **St. Gregory of Nazianzus, On His Father, 43**

135 This mortality is a bane to the Jews and pagans and enemies of Christ; to the servants of God it is a salutary departure. **St. Cyprian, Mortality, 15**

136 This is not an end, but a passage and, the journey of time being traversed, a crossing over to eternity. Would we not hasten to better things? **St. Cyprian, Mortality, 22**

137 Let us show that this is what we believe, so that we may not mourn the death even of our dear ones and, when the day of our own summons comes, without hesitation but with gladness we may come to the Lord at His call. **St. Cyprian, Mortality, 24**

138 Truly, honor for the dead does not consist in lamentations and moanings, but in singing hymns and psalms and living a noble life. **St. John Chrysostom, *Commentary on St. John the Apostle and Evangelist*, 2.177**

139 For the man who has departed this life will go on his way in the company of the angels, even if no one is present at his funeral. **St. John Chrysostom, *Commentary on St. John the Apostle and Evangelist*, 2.177**

140 The tombs of the saints occupy second place after the word in the power that they have to excite similar zeal in the souls of those who behold them. **St. John Chrysostom, *Discourse on Blessed Babylas*, 65**

141 Bury this body anywhere; let its care give you no concern. One thing only I ask of you, that, wherever you may be, you remember me at the altar of the Lord. **St. Augustine, *Confessions*, 8.11.27**

142 A costly funeral can do no more good for a villain than a cheap one—or none at all—can harm a saint. **St. Augustine, *City of God*, 1.12**

143 Although death is quite bitter to those who are alive, and quite troubling given the fact that someone has passed away, it is even more disturbing by the example it provides. As often as one sees a dead person, that often does he lament that he is defined to die. So a mortal cannot but grieve cornering death. **St. Peter Chrysologos, *Sermons*, 2.64.3**

144 For as long as men, these mortal and perishable creatures, exist and look upon the tombs of those from whom they came into being, they have grief inseparably joined to their lives, even if they take little notice of it. **St. Gregory of Nyssa, *On Virginity*, 3**

145 The experiences of living persons strengthen our faith in the words of the dead. **St. Gregory the Great, *Dialogues*, 4.58**

146 So, if we hold on to the true faith, if we harbor no doubts about the words of God, if we, with most certain hope, progress towards the future life, if we love God and neighbor worthily, if we do not await a vain glory from human beings but the true glory of the Christian name from God, we must not, like the unbelievers, have any sadness concerning the faithful departed and, to speak more precisely, our people who have fallen asleep. **Fulgentius, *Second Letter to the Widow Galla*, 3**

Rest and Freedom from Sin

147 Anyone who dies is said to be justified from sin. For a dead man does not lust or become angry or rage or rob what belongs to others. **Origen, *Commentary on the Epistle to the Romans*, 6.1.6**

148 So then, if we realize that our body can be put to death and become dead to sin, then it can come to pass that sin would not exercise dominion in it. **Origen, *Commentary on the Epistle to the Romans*, 6.1.6**

149 Without a doubt, the soul is purified when by the power of death it is released from the bondage to the flesh. **Tertullian, *On the Soul*, 53.6**

150 It is possible for us even here to live in happiness, and, on departing to the next world, to be freed from all sufferings and to attain to numberless blessings. **St. John Chrysostom, *Commentary on St. John the Apostle and Evangelist*, 1.414**

151 Death is not only not to the disadvantage of believers, but is even found to be to their advantage, for it removes a man from the risk of sinning and establishes him in the security of sinning no more. **St. Augustine, *On the Predestination of the Saints*, 14 (26)**

152 For what Christian would dare to deny that a just man, taken prematurely by death, shall find rest? **St. Augustine, *On the Predestination of the Saints*, 14.26**

153 You see, many people who in this present life fall on hard times and suffer injustice at the hands of their associates come to the end of their days without gaining any relief; so mighty David teaches them not to be annoyed, for the reason that death brings with it hope, and after death the recompense will be made. **Theodoret of Cyrus, *Commentary on the Psalms*, 4.8**

154 Now, David calls the life looked forward to "the land of the living" in so far as it is separated from death and free of corruption and sadness. **Theodoret of Cyrus, *Commentary on the Psalms*, 27.8**

155 Death is not an evil, since it is a refuge from all miseries and evils, a safe and secure anchorage, and a haven of rest. **St. Ambrose, *On His Brother Satyrus*, 2.22**

156 Therefore, let us pray that we too might stand in the temple, hold the Son of God, and embrace him, and that we might be worthy of release and of going on to better things. **Origen, *Homilies on Luke*, 15.5**

157 It is not so much having departed the world as having lived with the world that is full of sadness. **Braulio of Saragossa, *Letters*, 29**

158 Indeed, what we keep for our bodies in dissipation in this life we lose either during our lifetime, or at least immediately after our death. **St. Caesarius of Arles, *Sermons*, 14.1**

159 Through the power of the Word and separation from our old habits, we will obtain a benefit for our soul in death and the loss of prosperity. **St. Hilary of Poitiers, *Commentary on Matthew*, 10.26**

160 Anyone who departs from this world, anyone who is released from prison and the house of those in chains, to go forth and reign, should take Jesus in his hands. **Origen, *Homilies on Luke*, 15.2**

The Resurrection of the Body

161 If you believe that through God's power you can arise from death, you believe well. **St. Peter Chrysologos,** *Sermons***, 1.57**

162 Furthermore, after this death, which comes to all men and which is incumbent upon the descendants of the first man, hope for the final resurrection of your bodies. **St. Augustine,** *Sermons of the Liturgical Seasons***, 212.1**

163 He formed us out of nothing, and when hereafter we are dissolved, He will put us together again and deliver us to that other life, there to encounter either the fire, or God, the giver of light. **St. Gregory of Nazianzus,** *On His Own Affairs***, 542**

164 Therefore, our flesh will rise so that what shared in our virtue or guilt could also share in either reward or punishment. **St. Peter Chrysologos,** *Sermons***, 2.62.13**

165 The trumpet [which is the voice of God] which in the beginning called the world forth out of nothing, is the same one which on the last day will call the world back from destruction; and the trumpet which in the beginning raised the human being out of mud, is the same one that in the end will raise the human being up again out of dust. **St. Peter Chrysologos,** *Sermons***, 3.103.1**

166 Those who do not believe in the resurrection of the body mock us and our teaching that these bodies of ours rise again from the dead, considering it to be not only implausible but absolutely impossible. **Oecumenius,** *Commentary on the Apocalypse***, 11.9**

167 There are indeed many heretics who distort this faith in the resurrection. They claim that salvation is only for the soul and deny the resurrection of the body. But you who believe in Christ profess the resurrection of your body. **Niceta of Remesiana,** *Explanation of the Creed***, 11**

168 Treat this body with care, I pray you, and understand that with this body you will rise from the dead to be judged. **St. Cyril of Jerusalem, *Catechesis*, IV.28**

The Death of the Unbeliever

169 Look back on the end of each of the past emperors, and consider how they died the death common to all men, which, if it led to a state of insensibility, would be a godsend for all sinners. But since a state of sensibility does await all those who were alive ... be convinced and believe. **St. Justin Martyr, *First Apology*, 18**

170 For just as the senses perish at bodily death and the body no longer takes in either the sense of sight, hearing, smell, taste, or touch, so also is it that anyone who has ruined the spiritual senses in the soul neither sees God nor hears the words of God. **Origen, *Commentary on the Epistle to the Romans*, 4.5.10**

171 Therefore, death will die in us; but it will prevail in those who are condemned. **St. Augustine, *Sermons of the Liturgical Seasons*, 233.4**

172 It can be said that the first death, the death of the body, that it is good for saints and bad for sinners, but of the second death that it is certainly good for no one and non-existent for the saints. **St. Augustine, *City of God*, 13.2**

173 Never is a man worse off in death than when death itself is deathless. **St. Augustine, *City of God*, 13.11**

174 One should note that the fall is to the angels just what death is to men. For just as there is no repentance for men after their death, so there is none for the angels after their fall. **St. John of Damascus, *Orthodox Faith*, 2.4**

175 This confession [of the faith] will not be restrained by the gates of hell. It will not be bound by the chains of death. For that declaration is indeed a declaration of life. While it lifts those who confess it up to heaven, no less does it sink down into hell those who deny it. **St. Leo the Great, *Sermons*, 4.3**

Life after Death

176 There will be true life after death, and true comfort after desolation. **St. Augustine, *Letters*, 130, p. 380**

177 God promises immortality and eternity to you leaving this world, and do you doubt? **St Cyprian, *Mortality*, 6**

178 There is a nobler condition in store for us after our departure from this life. **St. John Chrysostom, *Commentary on St. John the Apostle and Evangelist*, 1.311**

179 We must rejoice a great deal over this transformation by which we are taken from earthly coarseness to heavenly dignity through the ineffable mercy of the one who descended to our state in order to lift us up to his. **St. Leo the Great, *Sermons*, 71.2**

180 The spirit which is not clothed with flesh is that of the angels. The spirit clothed in flesh, but not destined to die with it, is the human spirit. **St. Gregory the Great, *Dialogues*, 4.3**

181 The animal does not live on after death, while man begins to live only when he has completed his visible life through bodily death. **St. Gregory the Great, *Dialogues*, 4.4**

182 How will He be able to judge the dead? Why, those whom we regard as dead are living. **St. Peter Chrysologos, *Sermons*, 1.57**

183 Among mortals two gates towards hateful death are open. There are those who develop in their mind a turbid spring of evil. They are always concerned with presumptuous deeds, with the body, with wanton satiety, with hateful intrigues.... The others behold God with the pure eye of the mind. They hate pride, which is the shameless offspring of the world.... Their tree is lighter, for they are buoyed up by the Spirit as they follow the God who calls them. **St. Gregory of Nazianzus, *Concerning His Own Affairs*, 40–45**

Ending

184 Will not the spirit more clearly see all things
When in the grave its mortal vesture lies?

Aurelius Prudentius Clemens, *The Origin of Sin*, 920–21

185 When my poor soul has quit this mortal frame
Made up of sinews, skin, blood, gall, and bones,
To which, alas, its pampered inmate clings,
When death has closed these eyes, and cold I lie ...
To me be penance swift and merciful.

Aurelius Prudentius Clemens, *The Origin of Sin*, 941–44, 966

2

Judgment

Beginning

186 One God, Thy law directs and guides my life,
　　Thy judgment makes me tremble and grow pale;
　　Thy judgment makes me hope for pardon, too,
　　Unworthy though I be in words and deeds.

Aurelius Prudentius Clemens, *The Origin of Sin*, 932–35

God Delays His Judgment

187 God is a righteous judge, strong and long-suffering, who does not give free rein to his wrath every day. Instead, he also shows loving-kindness, by which he bears people's faults for a longer time.
Theodoret of Cyrus, *Commentary on the Psalms*, 7.6

188 The judgement of God is just, because it is delayed; because it is postponed repeatedly and for a long time, so that care and thought may be taken for man's eternal life by the long-enduring patience of God. **St. Cyprian, *The Good of Patience*, 4**

189 Many sins, likewise, seem now to be overlooked and visited with no punishments, but the penalties for these are reserved for the time to come; for it is not in vain that that day is called the day of judgment in which the judge of the living and the dead is to come. **St. Augustine, Faith, *Hope and Charity*, 17.66**

All Will Be Judged

190 An account is to be drawn up for each of us. There is no other time to give an account except the time of judgment. Then, what is entrusted to us, and what gains or losses we have made, will be clearly known. **Origen, *Homilies on Luke*, 35.11**

191 Admit that those whom the pagan world thinks have perished will arise again to be judged; that those who have died and will be found to be living may give an account both of their deeds and their life. **St. Peter Chrysologos, *Sermons*, 1.57**

192 Plato also stated that Rhadamanthus and Minos would punish the wicked who came before them. We declare that the very same thing will take place, but that it will be Christ who will assign punishment to sinners. **St. Justin Martyr, *First Apology*, 8**

193 We do not see that all of us must appear before the judgment seat of Christ, so that each one may receive either good or evil according to what he has done in the body. **Origen, *Homilies on Jeremiah*, 20.3.3**

194 Every man who seems negligible here on earth and not to be reckoned with, God sees him, however, and neither looks down upon him now nor will pass him by in His judgment. **St. Augustine, *City of God*, 20.2**

195 Praise has to be given on the day of judgment of him before whose tribunal all of us must stand, so that each one might receive recompense for what he has done in the body, whether good or evil. **Origen, *Homilies on Luke*, 2.7**

196 It is my opinion, in fact, that even if one could escape God's judgment, he ought not desire to. For not to come to God's judgment would mean not to come to correction, to the restoration of health and to that which heals. **Origen, *Commentary on the Epistle to the Romans*, 2.2.2**

197 For we shall all stand before God's tribunal to receive what we merit in Christ Jesus, to whom is glory and power for ages of ages. Amen. **Origen, *Homilies on Luke*, 2.7**

Judgment after Death

198 It is frightening, brothers, it is very frightening to hear these words, which reveal that after they die and once they have been consigned to penal custody in the underworld, such people are unable to be transferred to the peace of the saints, unless, now that they have been redeemed by the grace of Christ, they are set free from this desperate state by the intercession of the holy Church, so that what their sentence of condemnation refuses them, the Church may obtain, and grace may supply. **St. Peter Chrysologos, *Sermons*, 3.123.8**

199 Why don't you want to believe that souls are punished or rewarded in the meantime while awaiting the [final] judgment to glory or damnation? There they remain in hopeful confidence while anticipating their fate. **Tertullian, *On the Soul*, 58.2**

200 When we depart from the world and this life of ours has been transformed, some beings will be seated at the boundary of the world, as if they were exercising the office of tax collectors, very carefully searching to find something in us which is theirs. **Origin, *Homilies on Luke*, 23.5**

201   Yet, there must be a cleansing fire before judgment, because of some minor faults that remain to be purged away. **St. Gregory the Great, Dialogues, 4.41**

202   Now it is certain that the durations of punishment are determined according to the measure of sin and the delay of our conversion. **Origen, Homilies on Judges, 3.5**

203   An old man said: "I fear three things, that is, when my soul is going to depart from my body, and when I am going to come into the presence of God, and when the sentence is going to be pronounced against me." **Martin of Braga, Sayings of the Egyptian Fathers, 98**

The Last Judgment and the Resurrection

204   Scripture teaches us two things: first, that judgment will come; second, that it will be accompanied by the resurrection of the dead. **St. Augustine, City of God, 20.5**

205   We affirm that thou dost continue to exist after the extinction of life and to await the day of judgment; and that, according to thy deserts, thou wilt be delivered either unto torture or to bliss, both eternal. **Tertullian, Testimony of the Soul, 4**

206   And let not any one of you say this flesh is not judged and will not rise again. **Anonymous, So-called Second Letter of St. Clement to the Corinthians, 9.1**

207   You do not expect resurrection and judgment will take place? Even demons knowledge this fact. **St. John Chrysostom, Commentary on St. John the Apostle and Evangelist, 1.460**

208   John the Evangelist tells us with perfect plainness that Christ foretold that judgment was to come at the time of the resurrection of the dead. **St. Augustine, City of God, 20.5**

209   Let us say both to others and to ourselves as well: "There is a resurrection, and a fearful judgment awaits us." **St. John Chrysostom, *Commentary on St. John the Apostle and Evangelist*, 1.458**

210   When, however, we come to that judgment of God the proper name of which is "judgment day" or "the day of the Lord," we shall see that all His judgments are perfectly just: those reserved for that occasion, all those that He had made from the beginning, and those, too, He is to make between then and now. **St. Augustine, *City of God*, 20.2**

211   In connection with the last judgment, we who believe can be sure of the following truths: Elias the Thesbite will return; the Jews will believe; Antichrist will persecute the Church; Christ will be the judge; the dead will rise; the good will be separated from the wicked; the world will suffer from fire but will be renewed. **St. Augustine, *City of God*, 20.30**

212   As the Lord Himself teaches in the Gospel, the Day of Judgment will be at hand when the Gospel will have been preached in all the nations. **St. Augustine, *Commentary on the Lord's Sermon on the Mount*, 2.6.20**

213   He will judge both the living and the dead. For those will arise for judgment who are thought to be nonexistent after their death, and who in the opinion of the pagan world have perished utterly with the span of their life. **St. Peter Chrysologos, *Sermons*, 1.61**

214   For just as He, our Lord Jesus Christ, the Son of God, who is our Head, rose from the dead on the third day, so, too, do we hope that we who are His members shall rise in our flesh at the end of the world, that each may receive eternal rest or eternal punishment, according to what he has done in his body in this world. **Martin of Braga, *Reforming the Rustics*, 18**

215 He is the Resurrection, because He will raise all bodies from their graves; and the judge because it is He who will judge both the living and the dead. He is the door, because it is by Him that those who believe enter the Kingdom of Heaven. **Niceta of Remesiana, *Names and Titles of Our Savior***

216 Thus the judgment of God will be just, with both body and soul having a share either of retribution on account of sin or of virtue on account of religion and the future reward to be given to the saints. **St. Epiphanius of Cyprus, *Ancoratus*, 88.8**

217 If there is a resurrection and a judgment, there is no such thing as fate, even if some variously contend and put forth vigorous arguments that there is. **St. John Chrysostom, *Commentary on St. John the Apostle and Evangelist*, 1.459**

218 Believe that Christ Himself, our God, will come with the angels and the virtues of heaven to judge both the living and the dead, to give each according to his words, that is, to award eternal like to the just and to subject the wicked to eternal punishment. **Niceta of Remesiana, *Explanation of the Creed*, 6**

Faith and Judgment

219 And it is revealed that each person must be judged not by the privilege of possessing a certain nature, but by his own thoughts, accused or defended by the testimony of his own conscience. **Origen, *Commentary on the Epistle to the Romans*, 2.10.2**

220 Those unbaptized people who die confessing the name of Christ receive the forgiveness of their sins as completely as if they had been cleansed by the waters of baptism. **St. Augustine, *City of God*, 13.7**

221 One and the same baptism will be turned into condemnation and fire for the unworthy and for sinners; but to those who are holy and have been turned to the Lord in total faith, the grace of the Holy Spirit, and salvation, will be given. **Origen, *Homilies on Luke*, 26.3**

222 Those who think it sufficient for them to avoid evil usually say: If only I would merit to be found at the day of my death the same as I was when I went forth from the sacrament of baptism! Indeed, it is a fine thing for a man to be found cleansed from all evil on the day of judgement, but it is a grave wrong if he has not progressed in good works. **St. Caesarius of Arles, *Sermons*, 15.3**

223 Just as judgment still awaits a believer when he commits some sin in addition, though his faith is kept intact, so also the unbeliever shall not lose the remuneration for the good works he has done, his unbelief notwithstanding. **Origen, *Commentary on the Epistle to the Romans*, 2.7.7**

224 While time lasts, the reprobates, too, help to crowd our churches, but the winnowing fan will separate them from the elect on judgment's threshing floor. **St. Augustine, *City of God*, 18.48**

225 The same Cross of Christ brings glory to believers and punishment to unbelievers. **St. Leo the Great, *Sermons*, 60.2**

226 With so many sinners mingled with the saints, all caught in the single fishing net the Gospel mentions, this life on earth is like a sea in which good and bad fish caught in a net swim about indistinguishably until the net is beached, and the bad ones are separated from the good. **St. Augustine, *City of God*, 18.49**

227 Christ chose fishermen to be His Apostles, and changed fathers of fish into fishers of men, that fishermen's practice be recognized as a type of God's judgment.... Similarly, the vocation to the Christian faith brings together just and unjust, bad and good, but the divine election separates the good and the bad. **St. Peter Chrysologos, *Sermons*, 1.47**

228 Undoubtedly, he who is under the law of Christ will be judged by the law of Christ, and he who is under the law of Moses by the law of Moses. **Origen, *Commentary on the Epistle to the Romans*, 2.8.3**

229 In the Law, Abraham is in hell; in the Gospel, the robber is in heaven. **St. Jerome, *Homilies*, 76**

230 It is certain that if they do not believe, they will be condemned. **St. Augustine, *Letters*, 184A**

Preparing for Judgment

231 It pertains to one with great confidence and a pure conscience to ask for the kingdom of God without fearing the judgment. **St. Jerome, *Commentary on Matthew*, 1.6.10**

232 Therefore, let them, mindful of the judgment seat of Christ, examine their own conscience. **St. Basil, *Letters*, 223.2, p. 130**

233 For when I hear that dread sentence of God which is pronounced against him who transgresses through ignorance of even one commandment, I know not how to fear sufficiently the greatness of His wrath. **St. Basil, *On the Judgment of God* (*Ascetical Works*, p. 45)**

234 Let us then always be mindful of this tribunal, and thus we shall be able to persevere unceasingly in virtue. **St. John Chrysostom, *Commentary on St. John the Apostle and Evangelist*, 1.385**

235 Either let us fear the wrath which is to come or else let us love the grace we have—one or the other, so long as we are found in Jesus Christ unto true life. **St. Ignatius of Antioch, *Letter to the Ephesians*, 11**

236 As people, therefore, who are to present themselves in due time to the universal judge, let us adorn our souls with ever good work, let us renounce sensuality and corporal defilement. **St. Cyril of Alexandria,** *Festal Letter,* **26.4**

237 Let us gather imperishable treasure, treasures which can accompany us to heaven, can be our stay in danger, and render our judge merciful in that hour. **St. John Chrysostom,** *Commentary on St. John the Apostle and Evangelist,* **1.87**

238 By nothing else more than by showing compassion to our fellow man do we receive compassionate treatment in turn at the hands of Him who weighs mercy in his scale and balance and gives just recompense. **St. Gregory of Nazianzus,** *Selected Orations,* **14.5**

239 Therefore, regardless of however many other sins you have, your almsgiving counterbalances all of them. **St. John Chrysostom,** *On Repentance and Almsgiving,* **3.1**

240 Those who ask are forgiven, if they themselves forgive lesser amounts to those who sin. But if we refuse to be appeased for an insult that has been made, and if we have continual discord because of a word spoken too bitterly, does it not seem right that we should be led back to prison and that, based on the example of our conduct, no pardon should be granted to us for our transgressions? **St. Jerome,** *Commentary on Matthew,* **3.18.23**

241 Let us, then, lend Him our wealth so that we may receive pardon for our sins. For it is He Himself who acts as judge. **St. John Chrysostom,** *Commentary on St. John the Apostle and Evangelist,* **1.249**

242 The man who desires to reach the judgment free from anxiety must cast off everything burdensome. He who wants to possess heaven must despise the goods of the earth. **St. Valerian,** *Homilies,* **2.3**

243 Suppose there are some rich people who, though they are not in the habit of helping the poor in the Church with their largess, keep at any rate the commandments of God and figure that among the various meritorious activities of faith they are lacking but one virtue—and it is therefore a slight fault. Yet this one virtue happens to be so important that without it, the others cannot be of any avail. **St. Leo the Great, Sermons, 10.2**

244 Blessed is the one who discharges his debts to God, even when he does not know that he has incurred them, as the prophet instructs quite profoundly when he says: "At that time I restored what I did not take." **St. Peter Chrysologos, Sermons, 3.123.5**

245 As you see, dearly beloved, charity and the love of enemies are sufficient and more than enough to obtain the remission of sins, even if earthly riches be lacking. Therefore, we will have no excuse in the matter on the day of judgment. No one will be able to say that he did not have the means of redeeming his sins. **St. Caesarius of Arles, Sermons, 38.5**

246 O man, if you cannot be without sin, and wish your whole debt to be forgiven you always, you yourself should forgive always. **St. Peter Chrysologos, Sermons, 1.67**

247 We need to show great earnestness in all our affairs, beloved. And I say this because we shall give a reckoning, and we shall render a strict accounting both of our words and of our deeds. **St. John Chrysostom, Commentary on St. John the Apostle and Evangelist, 1.384**

248 But Matthew identifies himself as Matthew and as a tax-collector. He wants to show to his readers that no one should despair of salvation if he is converted to better things. **St. Jerome, Commentary on Matthew, 1.9.9**

249 That is why we continually insist on your being attentive and keeping awake so that nothing at all of what is said may escape you. In this way you may both live with much confidence now, and in that day stand confidently at the tribunal of Christ. **St. John Chrysostom, *Commentary on St. John the Apostle and Evangelist*, 1.110**

250 Unless the Church's pilots with all vigilance teach, terrify, sometimes even censure, and occasionally punish lightly, at times even threatening the day of judgment with severity, and thus show how to keep the straight path of eternal life, it is to be feared that they will receive judgment where they might have had a remedy. **St. Caesarius of Arles, *Sermons*, 1.19**

251 By ceaselessly proclaiming the rewards of the just and the punishment of sinners, we may arouse the good to better things and recall the wicked from their sinful actions through fear of future judgment. **St. Caesarius of Arles, *Sermons*, 1.5**

252 Let us now fear God as we ought, since He both sees what is happening now and punishes hereafter those who do not repent now. **St. John Chrysostom, *Commentary on St. John the Apostle and Evangelist*, 1.338**

253 We are thinking of the brevity of present things and the eternity of future things; how small the one is, how great the other. We think also of the future judge and the serious outcome of the tremendous judgment. **Salvian the Presbyter, *The Four Books of the Church*, 2.10**

254 Confession and reform do not come to the departed in Hades: God confined life and action to this life; there, however, he conducts an evaluation of performance. **Theodoret of Cyrus, *Commentary on the Psalms*, 6.5**

255 We fast. Do we thereby give God anything? We do it for our sins. We sleep on haircloth. What are we doing for the Lord in that? Only one thing; we are saving our souls, and that is what He desires. **St. Jerome, *Homilies*, 34**

256 Therefore, let prayer, mercy, and fasting be one petition for us before God. Let them be one legal aid in our behalf. Let them be a threefold prayer for us. These are the things, brethren, these are the things which hold fast the citadel of heaven, knock at the private chamber of God our Judge, follow up the cases of men before the Tribunal of Christ, beg indulgence for the unjust, win pardon for the guilty.
St. Peter Chrysologos, *Sermons*, 1.43

257 Abject in dress, in heart, reduced to silence, in my misery I challenge the pity of the King. He is benign to all the humble, but crushes the proud. **St. Gregory of Nazianzus, *On His Own Affairs*, 365**

258 Realize, o Christian, the dignity of your wisdom, and understand to what rewards you are called by the practice of such teaching. Mercy wants you to be merciful; justice wants you to be just. **St. Leo the Great, *Sermons*, 95.7**

259 Thus the Lord's preaching leads us up from the world to the light of the true sun. By the selection of those who are good and the rejection of those who are bad, it shows us the scrutiny of a future judgment.
St. Hilary of Poitiers, *Commentary on Matthew*, 13.9

260 We, however, have been taught that only they will have eternal bliss who live a holy and virtuous life close to God; we believe that they who live an evil life and do not repent will be punished by fire. **St. Justin Martyr, *First Apology*, 21**

261 If someone, then, thinks that he will not pay the price for his deceitful language, and does not expect to undergo bitter punishment for lying to God, then let him honor duplicity. **St. Cyril of Alexandria, *Festal Letter*, 9.5**

262 Who, therefore, would not with reason think that he may as well sin freely, if no judge were prescribing disciplinary measures for shameless, wicked deeds? **St. Valerian, *Homilies*, 1.3**

263 Because the ancient enemy makes use of these wiles, dearly beloved, Christ in his ineffable kindness wanted us to know what were the criteria for judging all humanity on the day of recompense. That way, while in this lifetime there is still available the medicine of legitimate remedies ... the condemnation due in justice might be headed off and the reflection of God's criteria in judgment might never be removed from the eyes of our heart. **St. Leo the Great, *Sermons*, 9.2**

264 Keep before one's eye that unsleeping eye and that incorruptible Tribunal, avoid becoming enthralled by money, be lavish in almsgiving, drive all ill-will to one's neighbor from the soul. **St. John Chrysostom, *Homilies on Genesis*, 8.14**

265 Be mindful of the judgment and neither fornication nor adultery nor murder nor any wickedness will prevail over you. **St. Cyril of Jerusalem, *Catechesis*, 2.2**

266 There is a middle mode of living, too sinful of itself to prepare a way to the kingdom of God, yet too full of services to the saints not to win their friendship and their grateful intercession for God's indulgence. **St. Augustine, *City of God*, 21.27**

267 We say we cannot do what we are unwilling to perform. I am certain that before the Tribunal of Christ this excuse will not exonerate us. **St. Caesarius of Arles, *Sermons*, 1.7**

268 Now someone may say: I lack memory, and have not the eloquence to preach the word of God. I am afraid, pious souls of the Lord, perchance this excuse will not be able to protect us at that dreadful judgment. **St. Caesarius of Arles, *Sermons*, 1.20**

269 What could be worse than this stupidity, though hearing every day about the judgment and the kingdom, we imitate those living in the time of Noah, and the people of Sodom, waiting to learn everything by experience? **St. John Chrysostom, *Commentary on St. John the Apostle and Evangelist*, 1.384**

270 Therefore, adversities neither straighten out the lazy nor overcome the strong, since it is neither one's material prosperity nor poverty, but one's character that either leads the grateful to their reward or leads the ungrateful away to their punishment. **St. Peter Chrysologos, Sermons, 3.124.2**

271 I beseech you, dearly beloved, and I exhort you with great humility that not one of you get angry at me or think that I am unreasonable or foolish when I frequently and purposely strive to impress upon you the fearful and dreadful day of judgment. **St. Caesarius of Arles, Sermons, 57.1**

272 Because the end of your life and the moment of death are coming; already attendants from heaven are ready to bind you, already judgment is beckoning; so hasten, in order not to lose time to make amends, you who have lost the time to do good deeds. **St. Peter Chrysologos, Sermons, 3.125.7**

273 When we accuse ourselves by our own confession and deny a consent of the heart to the carnal appetites … we build up an invincible peace with God. **St. Leo the Great, Sermons, 26.4.2**

274 Since we have such a lover of humanity as Judge, let us hurry to gain his favor, fulfilling endlessly Solomon's saying, "At all times my garments have been white," not being stained by evil deeds. **Andrew of Caesarea, Commentary on the Apocalypse, 3.21**

How We Are to Be Judged

275 These I confess; forgive and pardon me.
I merit punishment, but deign, good Judge,
To cancel what is due and freely grant
A better lot in answer to my prayers.

Aurelius Prudentius Clemens, The Origin of Sin, 937–40

276 We are treated very kindly, for it is in our power how we will be judged on the last day. **St. Caesarius of Arles, *Sermons*, 39.1**

277 To the degree we sin, the judgment on us grows, and if it mounts up to the stars, it is clearly for the holy ones. **Origen, *Fragments from the Catena*, 37**

278 Each one will have the weight of his good deeds hung in the balance, and for a few moments of a good work or a degenerate deed the scale often inclines to this side or that. **St. Ambrose, *Letters*, 15**

279 We believe that it is impossible for the wicked or the avaricious, or the treacherous, and the virtuous alike to hide from the sight of God, and that each man receives eternal punishment or salvation according to the merits of his actions. **St. Justin Martyr, *First Apology*, 12**

280 So, in the day of judgment, our works will either succor us or plunge us into the depths, like men weighted down with a millstone. **St. Ambrose, *Letters*, 15**

281 In truth, to the extent that we have transgressed in those things that we had promised to the devil, we will be handed over to the judge and to the officer and we will be cast into prison and we shall not come out from it until we pay back the last penny. **St. Jerome, *Commentary on Matthew*, 1.5.27**

282 Who can help but tremble at the thought of these judgments of God whereby He accomplishes whatever He pleases even in the hearts of wicked men, while yet rendering to each according to his merits? **St. Augustine, *Grace and Free Will*, 42**

283 For also with the measure that you measure will you be measured. Each person is responsible for himself for what is written.... You are responsible for yourselves if your name is to be inscribed in the heavens. **Origen, *Homilies on Jeremiah*, 17.4.5**

284 Whose hope reaches such a degree as to be bold enough to say "Measure your mercy by my hope"? Yet the Lord taught this even in the sacred Gospels: "The measure you use will be the measure applied to you." Consequently, let us acquire hope that is perfect and sincere, and keep the rest of our life in accordance with our hope, so as to reap much mercy. **Theodoret of Cyrus, *Commentary on the Psalms*, 33.9**

285 [It is not] as if those on the right would not have other virtues, those on the left other offenses! But at that great and ultimate judgment, the kindness of generosity or the ungodliness of avarice receives an extremely high value. **St. Leo the Great, *Sermons*, 10.2**

286 From your own conscience you will be judged, as your conflicting thoughts accuse or defend you, "on the day when God will judge the hidden secrets of men." **St. Cyril of Jerusalem, *Catechesis*, 15.25**

287 God is a searcher of the reins and heart and the observer and judge of hidden things; He sees and praises and approves you. **St. Cyprian, *Mortality*, 17**

288 For in God's judgment, even secret thoughts and unfulfilled violations can be accounted sinful. **Tertullian, *On the Soul*, 58.6**

289 How could anyone conceal his wrongdoing? Where shall we hide ourselves on the last day? Who will shelter us? How shall we escape the eye of God on the day when the purifying fire of God judges the deeds of all, and consumes the dry and crackling tinder of evil? **St. Gregory of Nazianzus, *On His Own Affairs*, 525**

290 But the heavenly Judge, who sees what is hidden, who hears what is unspoken, and who gets to the bottom of divergent testimony, considers it all from his divine perspective, evaluates it all in depth, and effortlessly determines what has been committed, but either bestows pardon on the one who confesses, or renders his sentence on the one who denies. **St. Peter Chrysologos, *Sermons*, 3.177.2**

291   And then God brings forth His judgment from the abasement of the judgment which raised itself so high from sin, by abasing the sin and rendering what is due.   **Origen, *Fragments from the Catena*, 37**

292   For on the day of judgment it is not possible, not at all, to counter the charge of negligence by babbling about having been oppressed and enslaved, when Christ, as it were, refutes and all but compels the law of freedom to shout down our explanations.   **St. Cyril of Alexandria, *Festal Letter*, 11.2**

293   The Devil longs to find something to charge us with before the tribunal of the eternal Judge and wants us to defend rather than to acknowledge our sins.   **St. Caesarius of Arles, *Sermons*, 59.1**

294   God carries out his own judgment in a humiliation of him whose judgment was exalted by sin.   **Origen, *Homilies on Jeremiah*, 28.12.4**

295   If the Lord prohibits judging, how is it consistent that Paul judges the fornicator in Corinth, and Peter convicts Ananias and Sapphira of lying? But from what follows he shows what he has prohibited. He says: for in what manner you judge, so shall it be judged concerning you. Thus he has not prohibited judging, but taught it.   **St. Jerome, *Commentary on Matthew*, 1.7.2**

296   For although men seem to have clear judgment, they cannot judge inerrantly. Both in praise and in censure, God alone is a just judge.   **Origen, *Homilies on Luke*, 2.4**

297   I am a judge, he says, and I do not make my decisions as a favor nor because people come forward to request or beg me. I distribute the prizes according to the outcome of the contests.   **St. John Chrysostom, *On the Incomprehensible Nature of God*, 8.38**

298 We are ignorant of the judgments of God and do not know the mysteries of each of his dispensations. **St. Jerome, *Commentary on Matthew*, 2.11.23**

299 The God of all looks down, not as ignorant and anxious to learn, but as judging and sentencing: how could the one who made the soul be ignorant of its movements? **Theodoret of Cyrus, *Commentary on the Psalms*, 33.7**

300 When His judgments are beyond our understanding, we should stand before them in awe, rather than with a questioning mind. **St. Gregory the Great, *Dialogues*, 4.27**

301 Your judgments are like the deep: possessing such wonderful truth and righteousness, why you show long-suffering I do not know; your judgments resemble the impenetrable depths. **Theodoret of Cyrus, *Commentary on the Psalms*, 36.4**

302 Who could doubt that this judgment-trial conducted by God is fair, when accusers, defenders and witnesses are summoned? **Origen, *Commentary on the Epistle to the Romans*, 2.10.1**

303 Just as judges in this life both punish the wicked and honor the just publicly, so will it be in the next world, so that the former will have greater shame, while the latter have more brilliant glory. **St. John Chrysostom, *Commentary on St. John the Apostle and Evangelist*, 1.459**

304 The Lord is one who tests what is just and he finds unworthy to test what is unjust, and is, shall I say, a banker of what is just and unjust. **Origen, *Homilies on Jeremiah*, 20.9.6**

305 In truth, sins are judged, not according to the time it took to commit them, but according to the very nature of the offenses. **St. John Chrysostom, *Commentary on St. John the Apostle and Evangelist*, 1.368**

306 The Lord has declared that on the day of judgment we shall give an account of every idle word. **St. Basil, *Letters*, 51.1, p. 134**

307 If we suffer chastisement on the day of judgment even for an idle word, there can be no doubt that we will have to render an account for innovation in matters of such great importance [as doctrine]. **St. Basil of Caesarea, *Against Eunomius*, 2.2**

308 If the judgment of sins committed in ignorance be so severe ... what should be said about those who knowingly commit sin? **St. Basil, *On the Judgement of God* (Ascetical Works, p. 45)**

309 The Savior will come this time, not to be judged, but to judge those who judged Him. **St. Cyril of Jerusalem, *Catechesis*, 15.1**

310 He who is now our Advocate, will then be our Judge.... How you would rejoice because he could be your judge who shortly before was your lawyer! **St. Augustine, *Sermons on the Liturgical Seasons*, 213.5**

311 If Christ judged the impious as God eternal and uncreated, everything would disappear; but acting with considerateness and not observing all the offenses of those under judgment, he acts as benefactor rather than punisher. **Didymus the Blind, *Commentary on Zechariah*, 2**

The Mercy of God

312 If the judgment of God, who renders precisely according to our deserts what is due to us for our deeds, should be by itself, what hope would there be? ... But as it is, "He liveth mercy and judgment." **St. Basil, *Exegetical Homilies*, 15, p. 233**

313 Every man, beloved brethren, hopes that when he comes to the day of judgment he will find mercy there. Now, if we all desire it, if all men want to find mercy in the future, let us make it our patron in this life that it may deign to welcome and defend us in the future. **St. Caesarius of Arles,** *Sermons,* **26.1**

314 Throw yourself upon God, and fear not; He will not pull Himself away and let you fall. **St. Augustine,** *Confessions,* **8.11.27**

315 "He fell upon his neck and kissed him." This is how the father judges the wayward son, and gives him not floggings but kisses. The power of love overlooks the transgressions. **St. Peter Chrysologos,** *Sermons,* **1.3**

316 It is as if He had made mercy a coadjutor to Himself, standing before the royal throne of His judgment, and thus he leads each one to judgment. **St. Basil,** *Exegetical Homilies,* **15, p. 233**

317 The Judge flung back onto himself his own sentence, so that he might show that he loves sinners more by paying the debt than by pardoning it. **St. Peter Chrysologos,** *Sermons,* **2.29.4**

318 Let us acknowledge our Savior; let us not fear our Judge. **St. Augustine,** *Sermons on the Liturgical Seasons,* **213.5**

319 When you are about to plead your case before the judgment seat of God, take mercy as your advocate, by means of which you can be freed. **St. Peter Chrysologos,** *Sermons,* **2.7.5**

320 He loves mercy, therefore, before judgment, and after mercy He comes to judgment. **St. Basil,** *Exegetical Homilies,* **15, p. 233**

321 God's mercy embraces the good with love, just as His severity corrects the wicked with punishment. **St. Augustine,** *City of God,* **1.8**

322 The fact also that God is angry does not arise from any vice in Him; rather He acts thus for our benefit. He is merciful even when He threatens, because by these threats men are recalled to the right path. **Novatian,** *The Trinity,* **5.4**

323   In short, if He sees that you are worthy of pity, He provides His mercy for you ungrudgingly.   **St. Basil,** *Exegetical Homilies,* **15, p. 233**

324   All the ways of the lord are mercy and truth, and we know that His grace can never be unjust nor His justice ever cruel.   **St. Augustine,** *City of God,* **12.28**

325   Whoever, presuming on his own justice, expects judgment with mercy as if he were secure, provokes the most just anger.   **St. Augustine,** *Letters,* **167.20**

326   In regard to the clemency of the Lord I say this, that Judas offended the Lord more by hanging himself than by betraying Him.   **St. Jerome,** *Homilies,* **35**

327   There are those among us ... who attribute to God even greater mercy.... The merciful God, they hold, will pardon the sinners by reason of the prayers of the saints.   **St. Augustine,** *City of God,* **21.18**

The Justice of God

328   Neither is mercy without judgment, nor judgment without mercy. **St. Basil,** *Exegetical Homilies,* **15, p. 233**

329   However, these qualities are joined to each other, mercy and judgment, lest either mercy alone should produce presumption, or judgment alone cause despair.   **St. Basil,** *Exegetical Homilies,* **15, p. 233**

330   God himself will seem to consequently pay back each person in accordance with his own good works; but evil should be understood to come not from God but from the evil juices of a lack of discipline and the blatant perverseness of one's deeds.   **Origen,** *Commentary on the Epistle to the Romans,* **2.6.3**

331   In truth, if God were not to be our judge, but we were to sit in judgment on ourselves, should we not cast the vote against ourselves? **St. John Chrysostom, *Commentary on St. John the Apostle and Evangelist*, 1.265**

332   Consequently, the whole human mass ought to be punished, and if the deserved punishment of damnation were rendered to all, beyond all doubt it would be justly rendered. **St. Augustine, *On Nature and Grace*, 5 (5)**

333   I well comprehend the severity of the judgment; for Our Lord says: "Unto whomsoever much is given, of him much will be required." **St. Basil, *On the Judgment of God* (*Ascetical Works*, p. 47)**

334   They are guilty before Him toward whom they have been ungrateful. **Tertullian, *Apology*, 40.12**

335   As a judge inflicts punishment on the criminal, still the cause of the punishment is not the justice of the judge, but the just retribution for the crime. **St. Augustine, *The Trinity*, 4.12.15**

336   But, if He sees your heart unrepentant, your mind proud, your disbelief in the future life, and your fearlessness of the judgment, then He desires the judgment for you. **St. Basil, *Exegetical Homilies*, 15, p. 233**

337   Nor is God unjust who condemns by the law of justice him who is made guilty by the law of sin. **St. Augustine, *Against Julian*, 4.9**

338   Thus, all the impious, by a true and just judgment of God, receive the same sufferings which they had inflicted. **Lactantius, *The Deaths of the Persecutors*, 50**

339   The Lord opens his treasury in the time of judgment, when the vessels of wrath are thrown out. **Origen, *Fragments from the Catena*, 33**

The Sentence Passed

340 There are two ways, one of life and one of death; and great is the difference between the two ways. *The Didache*, 1.1

341 This is my fear, and I live with it night and day. The thought of glory on the one side and punishment of the other does not let me breathe. **St. Gregory of Nazianzus, *On His Brother St. Caesarius*, 22**

342 But see the benevolent Lord mixing mercy with severity and weighing the degree of his punishment according to the balance of justice and mercy. **Origen, *Homilies on Judges*, 3.2**

343 The world to come is summer for the just, but it is winter for sinners. **The Shepherd of Hermas, *Parables*, 4th Parable, 2**

344 To be sure, this secret division is absolutely unknowable in this world of time, inasmuch as we have no certainty whether the man who is now upright is going to fall, or the man who is now lying flat is going to rise to righteousness. **St. Augustine, *City of God*, 20.7**

345 The judgment will be awesome, the sentence an occasion for dread. The kingdom of heaven lies before us, everlasting fire has been prepared. **St. Cyril of Jerusalem, *Catechesis*, 15.26**

346 Did you see his perfect judgment and how He gives both honor and punishment? He can award crowns and he can visit with vengeance. Some He leads into the kingdom and others He sends down into Gehenna. **St. John Chrysostom, *On the Incomprehensible Nature of God*, 8.7**

347 From the first man were to come all men, some to be associated with the bad angels in their punishment and others to be fellow citizens with the good angels in their reward. **St. Augustine, *City of God*, 12.28**

348 Indeed we have heard the irrevocable sentences: the one which the just will hear, never to depart from heaven; and the other which sinners will hear, never to leave hell. However, the kind and merciful Lord did not utter these sentences to lead us to despair, but to make us watchful and careful. **St. Caesarius of Arles, *Sermons*, 17.3**

349 For who but a fool thinks God unjust, whether in imposing penal judgment on whoever deserves it or in showing mercy to one who does not deserve it? **St. Augustine, *Faith, Hope and Charity*, 25.98**

350 The judgment of God is as harsh to the pitiless as it is kind to the merciful and, when those on the left have been thrown into the fire of hell for their inhumanity, the eternal blessedness of the heavenly kingdom will receive those on the right, praised for the generosity of their alms. **St. Leo the Great, *Sermons*, 45.4**

351 In the same fire, gold gleams and straw smokes; under the same flail the stalk is crushed and the grain threshed; the lees are not mistaken for oil because they issued from the same press. **St. Augustine, *City of God*, 1.8**

352 Therefore God is to be understood to hand over those whom he hands over, not that He himself would hand over anyone, but on account of the fact that He deserts unworthy persons, namely those who do not so improve themselves and cleanse themselves that God may gladly live in them. **Origen, *Homilies on Judges*, 2.5**

353 I observe that absolutely no pardon respecting any precept whatsoever is extended to those who do not repent of their disobedience. **St. Basil, *On the Judgment of God* (Ascetical Works, p. 52)**

354 How could they dare to say that they are being undeservedly condemned, that this sentence is being unjustly pronounced against them by so just a Judge? **St. Augustine, *Selected Sermons*, 60.10**

355   But he of whom it was foretold of old that he would come and would render a just and faultless decision in our regard has made gladness known to us no longer in its expectation but in its reality.   **St. Cyril of Alexandria, *Festal Letter*, 10.1**

356   For at that time there will be no room for impudence nor the capability of denying, since all the angels and the world itself will be a witness against sinners.   **St. Jerome, *Commentary on Matthew*, 3.22.11–12**

Ending

357   We hold that fires of that infernal night
In which souls stained by sin forever burn
The poor man sees from his abode;
Likewise the golden crows won by the just
Are shown across the intervening gulf
To souls confined in hell's dread prison house.
His ulcers healed, the soul in paradise
Beholds the torment of the reprobate,
And each has knowledge of the other's need.

Aurelius Prudentius Clemens, *The Origin of Sin*, 922–30

3

Heaven

Beginning

358 For He made Heaven first, about which he says "heaven is my throne." **Origen, *Homilies on Genesis*, I**

359 So, too, heaven was formed first, man last, as being a heavenly creature on earth. **St. Ambrose, *Letters*, 49, p. 257**

Desiring Heaven

360 He who is to come to the abode of Christ, to the glory of the heavenly kingdom, ought not to grieve and mourn, but rather, in accordance with faith in the truth, to rejoice at this departure and translation. **St. Cyprian, *Mortality*, 22**

361 Let us lament for our lawlessness so that we will appear to have offered some small thing, too. Because the things that will be given to us in the future are great and surpass our power. For it is paradise and the Kingdom of the Heavens. **St. John Chrysostom, *On Repentance and Almsgiving*, 3.23**

362   The City of God holds that eternal life is the supreme good and eternal death the supreme evil, and that we should live rightly in order to obtain the one and avoid the other. **St. Augustine, *City of God*, 19.4**

363   The one greatest good, then, is immortality, for the attainment of which we have been made from the beginning and for which we were born. We tend towards this. Human nature looks to this. Virtue carries us forward to it. **Lactantius, *The Divine Institutes*, 7.8**

364   We ought to rejoice and be of good heart, because, leaving behind this ephemeral life, we are going to another, much better and brighter, and one that is without end. **St. John Chrysostom, *Commentary on St. John the Apostle and Evangelist*, 2.83**

365   Life which is passed in temporal pleasures is not to be considered life but death in comparison with the eternal life promised to us through Christ and in Christ. **St. Augustine, *Letters*, 56, p. 294**

366   Having confidence in such a great promise, dearly beloved, be citizens of heaven not only in hope, but also in your daily life. **St. Leo the Great, *Sermons*, 4**

367   Do you see the unquenchable fire prepared for the demon, on the one hand, and for us, on the other hand, the kingdom, provided our resolve does not fail? **St. John Chrysostom, *Homilies on Genesis*, 17.25**

368   Even in the procuring of temporal goods, we should keep our mind on the kingdom of God, and in the service of the Kingdom, we should give no thought to temporal goods. **St. Augustine, *Commentary on the Lord's Sermon on the Mount*, 2.17.58**

369   Once we envision the choirs of angels, and fix our gaze on the company of saints and the majesty of an endless vision of God, the thought of having no part of these joys makes us weep more bitterly than the fear of hell. **St. Gregory the Great, *Dialogues*, 3.34**

370 Hence, those who seek earthly advantages in the Church do not set before their minds what God promises, for here there are temptations, dangers, and difficulties but He promises eternal rest and the companionship of the holy angels after these temporal sufferings. **St. Augustine, *Sermons on the Liturgical Seasons*, 252.6**

371 We belong to a different world far more sublime and abiding than the one you see around you. Our homeland is the Jerusalem above, the mighty and invisible, that no tyrant shall besiege or hope to subdue; our kinship is with the inspiration that we draw from the sons of virtue; our friends are prophets and patriarchs, on whom we peg our piety; our comrades are those who share our trials today, our peers in courage. **St. Gregory of Nazianzus, *Selected Orations*, 15.5**

372 As regards the hope of a future reward, any man who does not merely suppose but who knows, on the authority of infallible Truth, that he will enjoy, beyond the reach of evil and in the company of angels, union with the most high God is far happier in whatever state of physical sufferings he may be than the man who, even in the great delight of Paradise, was uncertain of his fall. **St. Augustine, *City of God*, 11.12**

373 He who prefers to live well in eternity will live badly in time and will be afflicted with all grievances and labors as long as he will be on earth, so that he may obtain divine heavenly solace. **Lactantius, *The Divine Institutes*, 7.5**

Heaven Open to Us

374 We were entrusted with paradise and did not prove worthy of our sojourn there, and yet He brought us to heaven. **St. John Chrysostom, *Commentary on St. John the Apostle and Evangelist*, 1.160**

375 As long as the earth remains, Heaven is not open; in fact, the gates are barred. When the world shall have passed away, the portals of paradise will be open. **Tertullian, *On the Soul*, 55.3**

376 The only key that unlocks the gates of paradise is your own blood … all other souls are kept in Hell until the Second Coming of the Lord. **Tertullian, *On the Soul*, 55.5**

377 From the time that our Lord suffered his passion down to the present day, this gate has been closed and been opened; closed to sinners and unbelievers, opened to the just and to believers. Through this gate, Peter entered, and Paul, and all the saints and martyrs; through this gate daily the souls of the just enter from every part of the world. **St. Jerome, *Homilies*, 93**

378 He ascended not to take Himself back to heaven—for He had always remained there—but rather to carry you there, whom He freed, bound as you were, and snatched away from hell. O man, understand whence and where God has raised you, in order to give a firm footing in heaven to you who on earth were on slippery footing and always liable to fall. **St. Peter Chrysologos, *Sermons*, 1.57**

379 The cross has taken away sin … it opened the gates of heaven, changed those who hated into friends; it took our human nature, led it up to heaven and seated it at the right hand of God's throne. **St. John Chrysostom, *Discourses against Judaizing Christians*, 3.4.7**

380 Nothing is more certain than that the souls of those who have attained perfect justice are received into the kingdom of heaven as soon as they leave the body. **St. Gregory the Great, *Dialogues*, 4.26**

381 Now the heavens are opened, not by an unbolting of the elements, but they are opened to the spiritual eyes, with which even Ezekiel at the beginning of his book records they were opened. **St. Jerome, *Commentary on Matthew*, 1.3.16**

382 The just will indeed see an increase in their reward on the day of judgment, inasmuch as up till then they enjoyed only the bliss of the soul. After the judgment, however, they will also enjoy bodily bliss, for the body in which they suffered grief and torments will also share in their happiness. **St. Gregory the Great, *Dialogues*, 4.26**

383 Christian people are invited to the wealth of Paradise, and the way has been thrown open to all believers for returning to their lost homeland—provided they do not close off for themselves that way which could be opened to the faith of a thief. **St. Leo the Great, *Sermons*, 66.3**

Gaining Entry to Heaven

384 You would not be wrong to call the churches on earth the gates of this [heavenly] city, through which it is possible to enter it: in them we are instructed and trained, and learn the way of life of that city.
Theodoret of Cyrus, *Commentary on the Psalms*, 87.2

385 If anyone desires to pass over to paradise after departing this life, and needs cleansing, Christ will baptize him in this river and send him across to the place he longs for. **Origen, *Homilies on Luke*, 9.2**

386 There are two gates: the gate of Paradise and the gate of the Church. Through the gate of the one, we enter the gate of the other.
St. Jerome, *Homilies*, 93

387 In fact there is no other ascent by which one may be raised up to heaven except through the Church of the manifold wisdom of God.
Origen, *Homilies on Judges*, 5.5

388 Holy men cannot obtain what has not been predestined. Whatever they accomplish through prayer has been predestined for accomplishment through prayer. Even our predestination to heaven has been so ordained that we must exert ourselves to attain it, for it is only through prayer that we obtain the kingdom decreed for us by God. **St. Gregory the Great, *Dialogues*, 1.8**

389 We are taught that all things must be perfectly and lawfully accomplished by those who have received the promise of the kingdom of heaven and that, if this perfect accomplishment be lacking, the gift of the kingdom is withheld. **St. Basil, *Concerning Baptism* (*Ascetical Works*, p. 353)**

390 For the grace of the Spirit gives eternal life and unspeakable joy in heaven, but it is the love of the toils because of the faith that makes the soul worthy of receiving the gifts and enjoying the grace. **St. Gregory of Nyssa, *On the Christian Mode of Life* (*Ascetical Works*, p. 131)**

391 Given God's graciousness, there are many opportunities for striving for eternity. Whenever we receive the righteous person and prophet in an attitude of reverence, we receive the honor attributed to the righteous and the prophet. **St. Hilary of Poitiers, *Commentary on Matthew*, 10.28**

392 Therefore, he receives an eternal share of the heavenly inheritance, who, preserving the unity of fraternal charity within the Catholic Church before he ends his present life, puts away the fatal hardness of an impenitent heart and does not despair. **Fulgentius, *On the Forgiveness of Sins*, 25.2**

393 But whoever behaves in such a way that he becomes worthy of the kingdom of heaven will receive what has been prepared, not for particular persons but for a particular kind of life. **St. Jerome, *Commentary on Matthew*, 3.20.23**

394 Such is the power of virtue, it makes man into an angel; it supplies the soul with wings to fly to heaven. **St. John Chrysostom, *On Repentance and Almsgiving*, 2.28**

395 With great readiness and hope, let us adhere to virtue and reveal the greatest repentance, so that, being freed here from all our sins, we can stand with courage before the Tribunal of Christ and be worthy of the Kingdom of the Heavens, in which may we all be found. **St. John Chrysostom, *On Repentance and Almsgiving*, 1.31**

396 When did an ease-loving farmer fill his barns? Who ever gathered in his harvest in the proper season if he did not first prepare the hard earth by many a furrow? The account taken of great virtue is this: the more a man works, the greater reward does he get. **St. Valerian, *Homilies*, 2.4**

397 The noblest enterprise is to purchase the kingdom of heaven for the price of a little blood and to trade ephemeral goods for eternal glory. **St. Gregory of Nazianzus, *Selected Orations*, 24.15**

398 In order to be great and fit for that kingdom, a man is bound to do and to teach as Christ is now teaching, so that his justice may exceed the justice of the Scribes and of the Pharisees. **St. Augustine, *Commentary on the Lord's Sermon on the Mount*, 1.9.21**

399 When we are wordy, we do not exalt God; but if from earthly beings we become heavenly beings, then we give glory to God. **St. Jerome, *Homilies*, 34**

400 Continually they praise You. Note the duty of the martyrs in heaven and of the angels. What they are doing in heaven, we accordingly imitate on earth. **St. Jerome, *Homilies*, 63**

401 Every man who is concerned to see God and attain to the heavenly kingdom can easily understand two facts: the requirements of the hard and narrow way have a bearing on the sum total of our life; and the hope of our getting to the glory of heaven lies in our effort. **St. Valerian, *Homilies*, 3.1**

402 I have no doubt that some who are taking part in the warfare which wins heaven experience a feeling of despair. It arises from this, that the very entrance to the laborious journey of the celestial warfare is distressingly narrow.... Lofty destinations are indeed vexatiously hard to attain, but, without doubt, travelers who refuse to despair do at length reach an open field. **St. Valerian, *Homilies*, 3.1**

403 Furthermore, the thief, after so much evil, entered into paradise before all others, because he did not become discouraged. **St. John Chrysostom, *On Repentance and Almsgiving*, 1.15**

404 Instead, he achieved righteousness by his humility. And in this way, he became worthy of the Kingdom of the Heavens, which may we all be worthy to attain. **St. John Chrysostom, *On Repentance and Almsgiving*, 2.29**

405 It might seem that [material] neediness alone, which many suffer in heavy and hard necessity, were enough to deserve the kingdom of heaven. But when he said, "Blessed are the poor in spirit," he showed that the kingdom of heaven is to be given to those whom humility of soul commends, rather than lack of means. **St. Leo the Great, *Sermons*, 95.2**

406 If the last day of his life shall find anyone in such progress and growth holding fast to the faith of the Mediator, he will be received by the holy angels, in order that he may be brought to the God whom he has worshipped, and by whom he is to be brought to perfection. **St. Augustine, *The Trinity*, 14.17.23**

407 And there are many such utterances which, if they were diligently read, would convince us even more firmly that we must comply with every prescription in order to merit the kingdom of heaven. **St. Basil, *Concerning Baptism* (*Ascetical Works*, p. 354)**

The Reward of the Saints

408 A beautiful crown of flowers that never fade await those who live well; earth has never been capable of bearing such a crown, for only heaven holds the secret of bringing it to blossom. **Clement of Alexandria, Christ the Educator, 8.73**

409 What will be the glory and how great will be the joy to be admitted to see God … to rejoice with the just and with the friends of God in the kingdom of heaven in the delight of immortality bestowed, to receive there what "eye has not seen nor ear heard." **St Cyprian, Letters, 58.10**

410 Here on earth, no one has ever seen it. But those who are there in heaven constantly behold their king. They can see Him in their midst and there can also see how He sheds on all who are gathered there the brightness of His own glory. **St. John Chrysostom, On the Incomprehensible Nature of God, 6.9**

411 Now [a saint] is an inhabitant of the regions above, an occupant of the eternal city Jerusalem, which is in heaven. He sees there that city's boundless boundary, its pure gold, its precious stone, its perpetual light which knows no sun. **St. Ambrose, Letters, 37, p. 201**

412 The number pertains to the saints who are destined to reign with Christ. Now persons can enter the Church in excess of that number; they cannot so enter the kingdom of heaven. **St. Augustine, Sermons on the Liturgical Seasons, 251.2**

413 It has pleased the Divine Providence to prepare for the just joys in the world to come in which the unjust will have no part. **St. Augustine, City of God, 1.8**

414 Now, as for what the Lord says: "To sit at my right and my left is not mine to give to you, but to those for whom it has been prepared by my Father," this should be understood in the following manner: the kingdom of heaven does not belong to the one giving but the one receiving, "for there is no receiving of persons with God." **St. Jerome, *Commentary on Matthew*, 3.20.23**

415 God gives the Kingdom of Heaven, with its happiness, only to those who believe in Him, while he gives the earthly city to both believers and unbelievers alike. **St. Augustine, *City of God*, 5.21**

416 After the Lord had warned them that they had to take up the cross, lose their lives, and exchange the loss of the world for eternal life, he turned to the disciples and said that there would be some among them who were not going to taste death until they behold the Son of Man in the glory of his Kingdom. **St. Hilary of Poitiers, *Commentary on Matthew*, 17.1**

417 The crown of victory is promised to those who engage in the struggle. **St. Augustine, *The Christian Combat*, 1.1**

Almsgiving and Heaven

418 There are three levels of living: one so evil that those who lead it can be helped into the Kingdom of Heaven by no amount of almsgiving; another good enough to make possible the obtaining of beatitude; and a third between these two, a middle kind of life standing in need of the merits of those whom they have befriended by their alms that mercy may be obtained. **St. Augustine, *City of God*, 21.27**

419 Dearly beloved, those possessions, increased through our worldly deeds, are our misfortunes. While devoting too much attention to them, many men have lost the goods of heaven. **St. Valerian, *Homilies*, 2.2**

420 It is a dangerous matter to want riches when innocence is violated by the heavy burden of being occupied with accumulating wealth. On the contrary, serving God is not pursuing the things of the world without [also sharing] in the sins of this world. For this reason it is difficult for a rich man to enter the kingdom of heaven. **St. Hilary of Poitiers, Commentary on Matthew, 19.9**

421 To keep a man from sharing in the heavenly kingdom, the Devil puts gold in his hands, silver before his eyes, gems around his neck. **St. Valerian, Homilies, 7.3**

422 Therefore, do not let your heart be hardened; extend a coin to Christ, from whom you desire to receive a kingdom. **St. Caesarius of Arles, Sermons, 26.5**

423 While it allures the rich man to take too much pleasure in his excessive store of money, it excludes him from the kingdom of heaven. **St. Valerian, Homilies, 2.6**

424 Clearly it is better to carry the gold of the abode of the soul than to bury the soul in the one of the gold. That is why God orders those who will serve in His army here below to fight as men stripped of concern for riches and unencumbered by anything. To these He has granted the privilege of reining in heaven. **St. Peter Chrysologos, Sermons, 1.22**

425 Hear him as he passes judgment on those at his right hand: "You saw me hungry and gave me to eat; you saw me thirsty and gave me to drink; you saw me naked and covered me." **St. John Chrysostom, Discourses against Judaizing Christians, 3.5.4**

426 They are to possess the kingdom because, like good and faithful Christians, they did not disregard the Lord's words, but gave alms, and did so with the confident hope of receiving the promised rewards. **St. Augustine, Selected Sermons, 60.9**

427 The kingdom of heaven does not apply force, nor does it exact tribute, but it welcomes those who freely offer their goods. **St. Basil, On Mercy and Justice (Ascetical Works, p. 512)**

428 Therefore, brethren, you will enter the kingdom of heaven, not because you have not sinned, but because you have redeemed your sins by almsgiving. **St. Augustine, *Selected Sermons*, 60.10**

429 It is in return for our care of the poor so regarded that we are to be admitted into fellowship with the kingdom of heaven. **St. Leo the Great, *Sermons*, 9.3.2**

430 Look, possession of the kingdom of heaven is now offered to you, and for a very low price. Anyone not accustomed to allege his poverty as a pretext can easily buy this possession. **St. Valerian, *Homilies*, 7.4**

431 Have you already forgotten what the Lord is going to say to those who have given alms to the poor: "Come, blessed of my Father, take possession of the Kingdom"? **St. Augustine, *Sermons of the Liturgical Seasons*, 198.2**

432 So if anyone desires to find a place in the heavenly abode, let him not cease to dispense the necessities of life to the indigent. **St. Valerian, *Homilies*, 7.3**

433 Turn our souls to the healing of repentance and the remedies of almsgiving, [so that] we will happily come before the Tribunal of Christ to be crowned not condemned. **St. Caesarius of Arles, *Sermons*, 18.7**

434 We need only the poor, the maimed, the crippled, the sick.... These dispatch our wealth to heaven. **St. John Chrysostom, *Commentary on St. John the Apostle and Evangelist*, 1.160**

435 If we compare heavenly things with earthly, it is evident that something very valuable is for sale at a rather low price. How great is your alms in proportion to all the things which the Lord has clearly promised to mortal men? **St. Valerian, *Homilies*, 7.6**

436 So let us now follow the Word; let us seek the repose on high; let us cast aside the opulence of this world; let us have recourse to only that portion of it that serves a good end; let us gain our lives by acts of charity; let us share the wealth we have with the poor that we may be rich in the bounty of heaven. **St. Gregory of Nazianzus, *Selected Orations*, 14.22**

437 If, then, you wish the gate of heaven to open for you, you must give up all your goods. **St. Valerian, *Homilies*, 2.3**

438 If I do not give alms, am I excluded from the number of the just? Not at all, for how many holy people have given alms and fallen from sanctity! The perfect have not given alms; they have none to give. To have no part in almsgiving is a reproach to the man of possessions; but the man who possesses nothing from which to give alms is free.
St. Jerome, *Homilies*, 38

439 One angel was not enough to carry the pauper, but many came to form a chorus of jubilation. Every angel rejoices to touch so precious a burden. With pleasure, they bear such burdens in order to conduct men into the kingdom of heaven. **St. Jerome, *Homilies*, 86**

440 Let us offer to him through the poor who are today downtrodden, so that when we depart this world they may receive us into the eternal habitations in Christ himself, our Lord, to whom be the glory forever.
St. Gregory of Nazianzus, *Selected Orations*, 14.40

441 Give bread and seize paradise. **St. John Chrysostom, *On Repentance and Almsgiving*, 3.8**

442 The kingdom of the Heavens, paradise, and the goods "that no eye has seen, nor ear heard, nor heart of man conceived ..." are all set before us. Are we not obliged to do all we can in order to offer something, so that we will not be deprived of these goods? **St. John Chrysostom, *On Repentance and Almsgiving*, 3.22**

443 If you wish to live eternally in that good place where no one is hungry, now in this evil place break your bread with the hungry. **St. Augustine, *Sermons on the Liturgical Seasons*, 217.2**

444 What is necessary? Not to be evil; is that sufficient in itself? ... Give whatever sum you wish to the poor. Then you will be entertaining Christ in a worthy fashion. **St. Gregory of Nazianzus, *On Himself and Bishops*, 454–61**

Describing Heaven

445 To tell the truth, I have no real notion of what eternal life would be like, for the simple reason that I know of no sensible experience to which it can be related. **St. Augustine, *City of God*, 22.29**

446 It is not that I am unable to write to you of heavenly realities, but I am afraid that, children as you are, I might do you harm. **St. Ignatius of Antioch, *Letter to the Trallians*, 5**

447 When you hear that we look forward to a kingdom, you rashly assume that we speak of a human kingdom, whereas we mean a kingdom which is with God. **St. Justin Martyr, *First Apology*, 11**

448 I seem to be possessed by an unusual eagerness in my quest to clarify the facts about Paradise, its place, and its nature to those who are desirous of this knowledge. **St. Ambrose, *Paradise*, 1**

449 The passing and impure things of earth cannot approach the immortal purity of Heaven. **St. Augustine, *City of God*, 9.17**

450 This peace which is promised to the blessed is called a river to help us to realize that, in the land of felicity which is in heaven, everything will be, as it were, soaking in perfect beatitude. **St. Augustine, *City of God*, 20.21**

451 "Life everlasting." This faith, this mystery, is not something to be consigned to note paper or written by letters, because papers and letters remind us of objects to be cared for more than grace. **St. Peter Chrysologos, *Sermons*, 1.57**

452 To us uncouth newcomers the unfamiliar felicity of heaven will seem like a mother's tenderness and care. There we shall see and our heart will rejoice. **St. Augustine, *City of God*, 20.21**

453 Paradise is, therefore, a land of fertility—that is to say, a soul which is fertile. **St. Ambrose, *Paradise*, 12**

454 Heaven, too, will be the fulfillment of the Sabbath rest foretold in the command: "Be still and see that I am God." **St. Augustine, *City of God*, 22.30**

455 In this city, Christ reigns; in this city, the inhabitants themselves are both dwellers and gates, both houses and dwellers. Would you know how they are houses? Christ dwells in them; Christ moves about in them. **St. Jerome, *Homilies*, 46**

456 Who can imagine, let alone describe, the ranks upon ranks of rewarded saints, to be graded undoubtedly, according to their variously merited honor and glory. Yet there will be no envy of the lower for the higher. **St. Augustine, *City of God*, 22.30**

457 But you, sacred and holy soul, may you enter heaven, may you rest in Abraham's bosom—whatever may be the meaning of this—may you behold the chorus of angels and the splendors and glories of blessed men. **St. Gregory of Nazianzus, *On His Brother St. Caesarius*, 17**

458 This is the kingdom of God, when no other will that God's prevails, either in heaven or on earth; when in the case of all men, God is the directing mind, God is living, God is acting, God is reigning, God is everything, so that, according to that statement of the Apostle: "God may be all in all of you." **St. Peter Chrysologos, *Sermons*, 1.67**

Heaven Is Physical

459 After saying "your heart shall rejoice," Isiah added, "and your bones shall flourish like an herb." Hence we are not to think that the joys of the heavenly Jerusalem are limited to the spirit. **St. Augustine, City of God, 20.21**

460 The heavens are the outer shell which contains both visible and invisible created things. For, enclosed and contained within them are the spiritual powers, which are the angels, and all sensible things. Only the Divinity is uncircumscribed, flying, containing, and surrounding all things, because He transcends all things and it is He who has created all. **St. John of Damascus, Orthodox Faith, 2.6**

461 In size the heavens are much greater than the earth. Nevertheless, one must not inquire into the substance of the heavens, because we can know nothing about it. **St. John of Damascus, Orthodox Faith, 2.6**

462 All heaven is [a] tomb to him who lacks a grave. **St. Augustine, City of God, 1.13**

463 Accordingly, we learn there is a heavenly city of some kind, called Jerusalem, with no towers or ramparts nor gleaming with sparkling stones, but conspicuous for choirs of saints and adorned with an angelic way of life. **Theodoret of Cyrus, Commentary on the Psalms, 87.2**

Our Heavenly Bodies

464 Man was an animal made out of earth, but not unfit for heaven, if only he would remain close to his Creator. **St. Augustine, City of God, 22.1**

465 The saints will see God with their bodily senses, but whether they will see Him by their sense in the same way we now see the sun and moon and stars, the land and the sea and all they contain—that is a difficult problem. **St. Augustine, *City of God*, 22.29**

466 It is difficult to admit that bodies in heaven will be such that the saints cannot open and close their eyes at will; on the other hand, it is still harder to admit that, if one closes his eyes in heaven, he will cease to see God. **St. Augustine, *City of God*, 22.29**

467 When we speak of eyes in heaven having a more powerful vision, we do not mean the kind of sharper sight which snakes and eagles are said to have.... What is meant is that in heaven eyes can see realities that are immaterial. **St. Augustine, *City of God*, 22.29**

468 [In heaven] we see no garments or cloaks but we see crowns more valuable than any gold, than any contest prizes or rewards, and ten thousand blessings stored up for those who live upright and virtuous lives on earth. **St. John Chrysostom, *On the Incomprehensible Nature of God*, 6.7**

469 The bodies of the saints, such as they will be in the resurrection, will have no need of the fruit from any tree to save them from dying from any ailment or inveterate old age, nor will they have need of other material food or drink to protect them against the pangs of hunger or the pain of thirst, for the saints will be robed in bodies so adorned with the certain and utterly inviolable gift of immortality that they will feel no need to eat, although able to do so if they choose. **St. Augustine, *City of God*, 13.22**

470 In this community, God is the life by which the spirits live. He is the food on which their blessedness is fed. **St. Augustine, *City of God*, 22.1**

471 These movements of our bodies [in heaven] will be of such un-imaginable beauty that I dare not say more than this: There will be such poise, such grace, such beauty as becomes a place where nothing unbecoming can be found. **St. Augustine, *City of God*, 22.30**

Who Is in Heaven

472 It is to the gentle and the mild, to the humble and the unassuming, and to those prepared to bear all injuries that the earth is promised. This must not be considered a small or contemptible inheritance, as if it were separated from the heavenly home, for these are the very ones who are understood to enter the kingdom of heaven. **St. Leo the Great, Sermons, 95.5**

473 For the righteous man is also heaven. **Origen, Homilies on Jeremiah, 8.2**

474 Having overcome the unjust ruler by his endurance and thus having gained the crown of immortality, he rejoices with the Apostles and all the just saints and is glorifying God, the Almighty Father, and blessing our Lord Jesus Christ. **The Martyrdom of St. Polycarp, 19.2**

475 Those who die this new death for God, and violently as Christ did, are welcome into a special abode. **Tertullian, On the Soul, 55.5**

476 The crowns of martyrs await you, brothers; the choirs of confessors are ready to reach out to you their hands and to receive you into their number. **St. Basil, Letters, 139; 1, p. 285**

477 Those in heaven, indeed, merit to be called happy, not to be pitied. **St. Basil, Exegetical Homilies, 15, p. 234**

478 In heaven the throngs which come together are much larger, holier, and more august. **St. John Chrysostom, On the Incomprehensible Nature of God, 6.8**

479 Nor are the crowds [of heaven] made up of city dwellers or country folk. Instead, in one place in heaven, we find myriads of angels, in another place, thousands of archangels, elsewhere, companies of prophets, in another place, choirs of martyrs, battalions of just men, and many

various groups of people in whom the Lord has been well pleased.
St. John Chrysostom, *On the Incomprehensible Nature of God*, 6.8

480 This is a goodly plantation for angels and saints. The saints are
said to lie beneath the fig tree and the vine. **St. Ambrose, *Paradise*, 2**

481 The first man in Paradise was more fortunate than any saint now
subject to weakness and mortality. **St. Augustine, *City of God*, 11.12**

482 Happy the man who has merited to be on the fifteenth step in the
heavenly Jerusalem and in the temple! Because that height is so sublime and is, I think, the place of the apostles and the holy martyrs, let
us pray that we may merit to be at least on the lowest step of the temple
of the Lord. **St. Jerome, *Homilies*, 41**

483 The angels indeed see the heavenly Jerusalem being constructed
from all the nations of the world. How much should the lowliness of
human beings rejoice over this indescribable work of divine pity when
the sublimity of angels so delights in it? **St. Leo the Great, *Sermons*, 21.2**

484 The good rejoice the more to see their loved ones in happy eternity
with them.... But there is something even more wonderful in store
for God's chosen ones. They will recognize not only those whom they
knew on earth, but many saintly men and women whom they had never
seen before will appear to them as old friends. And so, when they meet
the saints of the ancient past, they will not appear unfamiliar to them,
for they always knew them through their deeds. **St. Gregory the Great,
Dialogues, 4.34**

485 On account of the great goodness of the one who founded the holy
city of Jerusalem, it is inhabited by people of the kind who not only
are motivated in action and thought by reason but also are simple in
their tastes and of a lowly attitude. **Didymus the Blind, *Commentary on
Zechariah*, 2**

The Heavenly Life

486 The kingdom of heaven, then, must be contemplation. **St. Basil, Letters, 8; I, p. 38**

487 In heaven we find no wheat, no barley, no different kinds of products. But we do find everywhere in heaven love, the first fruit of the Spirit. **St. John Chrysostom, *On the Incomprehensible Nature of God*, 6.7**

488 [In Heaven], your neighbor is going to have knowledge of what you know you are thinking. **St. Augustine, *Sermons on the Liturgical Seasons*, 243.5**

489 The saints behold God with a clarity common to all. Why, then, should anything be unknown to them in heaven where they know God, the all-knowing? **St. Gregory the Great, *Dialogues*, 4.34**

490 [In heaven] we find joy and pleasure and peace and goodness and mildness in great abundance. **St. John Chrysostom, *On the Incomprehensible Nature of God*, 6.7**

491 The way of life in heaven, removed from all despondency, is characterized by joy and satisfaction, pure and unalloyed. The devotees of piety, far from merely sojourning there, dwell forever. **Theodoret of Cyrus, *Commentary on the Psalms*, 87.5**

492 There are no flocks of sheep or herds of cattle. But, to be sure, the spirits of just men who have been made perfect, the goodness of souls, and the virtuous deeds of men whose characters are sound can be seen everywhere in heaven. **St. John Chrysostom, *On the Incomprehensible Nature of God*, 6.7**

493 We shall see the truth there without any difficulty, and shall enjoy it to the full because it is most clear and most certain. **St. Augustine, *The Trinity*, 15.25.44**

494 Festivals here on earth often end at noon. Not so the festal assembly in heaven. Nor does that festival wait for the months to return in their cycle. **St. John Chrysostom,** *On the Incomprehensible Nature of God,* **6.10**

495 The festival in heaven continues with no interruption. Its blessings have no limit, the feast itself knows no end. **St. John Chrysostom,** *On the Incomprehensible Nature of God,* **6.10**

496 In heaven, all glory will be true glory, since no one could ever err in praising too little or too much. **St. Augustine,** *City of God,* **22.30**

497 [In heaven] voices rise in rhythmic harmony, as if blending with the lyre in the sweetest music, to praise the master who created heaven and earth. **St. John Chrysostom,** *On the Incomprehensible Nature of God,* **6.10**

498 In heaven there is no tumult or disturbance such as on earth. There everything is in proper order and well arranged. **St. John Chrysostom,** *On the Incomprehensible Nature of God,* **6.10**

499 They all stand on divergent steps [in the heavenly temple], to be sure, but in unison they sing one psalm of praise and thanksgiving to the Lord. Places vary, but the praise of the Lord is one. **St. Jerome,** *Homilies,* **41**

500 Just as there is life there in heaven, so there is watchfulness without end. **St. Augustine,** *Sermons of the Liturgical Seasons,* **221.3**

Free Will without Sin

501 [In heaven] there will be no need for reason to govern non-existent evil inclinations. God will hold sway over man, the soul over the body;

and the happiness in eternal life and law will make obedience sweet and easy. **St. Augustine,** *City of God*, **19.27**

502 In that final peace which is the end and purpose of all virtue here on earth, our nature, made whole by immortality and incorruption, will have no vices and experience no rebellion from within or without. **St. Augustine,** *City of God*, **19.27**

503 The souls in bliss will still possess the freedom of will, though sin will have no power to tempt them. They will be more free than ever—so free, in fact, from all delight in sinning as to find, in not sinning, an unfailing source of joy. **St. Augustine,** *City of God*, **22.30**

504 Our will will be as ineradicably rooted in rectitude as love is in beatitude. **St. Augustine,** *City of God*, **22.30**

505 In the everlasting City, there will remain in each and all of us an inalienable freedom of the will, emancipating us from every evil and filling us with every good, rejoicing in the inexhaustible beatitude of everlasting happiness, unclouded by the memory of any sin or of sanction suffered, yet with no forgetfulness of our redemption or any loss of gratitude for our Redeemer. **St. Augustine,** *City of God*, **22.30**

The Eternity of Heaven

506 What pleasure there is in the heavenly kingdom without fear of death, and with an eternity of life the highest possible and everlasting happiness. **St. Cyprian,** *Mortality*, **25**

507 On that last day, we shall rest and see, see and love, love and praise—for this is to be the end without end of all our living, that Kingdom without end, the real goal of our present life. **St. Augustine,** *City of God*, **22.30**

508 In the eternal City of God, each and all of the citizens are personally immortal with an immortality which the holy angels never lost and which even human beings can come to share. **St. Augustine, *City of God*, 22.1**

509 Such is the house of God, not earthly or corporeal as formed from any celestial substance with mass, but spiritual and a participant in Thy eternity, because without stain forever. **St. Augustine, *Confessions*, 12.19**

510 What is everlasting life if not "that they may know Thee, the only true God and Him who Thou has sent"? **St. Augustine, *The Trinity*, 1.12.31**

511 Whatever will be there will be good, and the supreme God will be the supreme good, and He will be present for the enjoyment of those who love Him; and the culmination of all this blessedness will be the certainty that it will be so forever. **St. Augustine, *The Trinity*, 13.7.10**

512 These who have been during their lives faithful and good shall enter the kingdom of God with His holy angels, and their souls shall be reunited with their flesh in eternal rest, nevermore to die, where there shall be no labor and no pain, no sorrow, no hunger nor thirst, no heat nor cold, no darkness nor night; but ever happy, satisfied, in light, in glory, they shall be like the angels of God, because they have deserved to enter that place from which the devil and his angels who conspired with him fell. **Martin of Braga, *Reforming the Rustics*, 14**

Those in Heaven Know of Hell

513 In virtue of the vigor of their minds, [the saints in heaven] will have not merely a notional remembrance of their own past but also a knowledge of the unending torments of the damned. **St. Augustine, *City of God*, 22.30**

Ending

514   Thy father's house has mansions manifold,
        O Christ. I do not ask Thee for a home
        In regions of the blest; let those chaste throngs
        Dwell there, who scorning things of earth, have sought
        Thy riches, and virgins innocent,
        Who have renounced carnal appetites.
        Enough that I behold no slave of hell.

Aurelius Prudentius Clemens, *The Origin of Sin*, 952–58

4

Hell

Beginning

515 What did God do before he made heaven and earth? Some jest that He was preparing Hell for those who pry into such deep questions! **St. Augustine, *Confessions*, 11.12.14**

What Is Hell?

516 It is better to escape eternal punishment than to learn its nature. **St. Augustine, *Commentary on the Lord's Sermon on the Mount*, 1.11.30**

517 What is the abyss? That place, of course, where the Devil and his angels will be. **Origen, *Homilies on Genesis*, 1.1**

518 We Christians do not consider Hell to be an empty cavern or some subterranean sewer of the world. **Tertullian, *On the Soul*, 55.1**

519 In our churches we hear countless discourses on eternal punishments, on rivers of fire, on the venomous worm, on bonds that cannot be burst, on exterior darkness. **St. John Chrysostom, *Discourses against Judaizing Christians*, I.IV.1**

520 Some men mislead themselves, saying that the eternal fire spoken of is not the same as eternal punishment, for they think that those to whom they promise salvation through fire, because of their deep faith [without works], will surely pass through. **St. Augustine, *Eight Questions of Dulcitius*, Question 1**

Why Hell Was Made

521 What God is saying is this: I have made ready the kingdom for men. But it was not for men that I prepared Gehenna but for the devil and his angels. **St. John Chrysostom, *On the Incomprehensible Nature of God*, VIII.8**

522 What could be more pitiable than the fate of those people who on account of neglect of their own salvation make themselves liable to that punishment prepared for that demon? **St. John Chrysostom, *Homilies on Genesis*, 17.25**

The Justice of Hell

523 Surely, just as sin is unjust, the punishment for sin is just.
St. Augustine, *Continence*, 6.15

524 Almighty God, being a God of love, does not gratify His anger by torturing wretched sinners. However, since He is a God of justice, the punishment of the wicked cannot satisfy Him even if it continues eternally. **St. Gregory the Great, *Dialogues*, 4.46**

525 The full justice of the Judge, therefore, demands that the wicked, who never wished to be rid of sin during life, should never be without punishment in eternity. **St. Gregory the Great, *Dialogues*, 4.46, 792**

526 You confess the torment—confess then that it is deserved.
St. Augustine, *Against Julian*, 12.24

527 If we understand the "prison" of which the Gospel speaks, as Hell, and the "last farthing" as the smallest defect that has to be atoned for there before the resurrection, there will be no doubt that the soul suffers in Hell some retributory penalty. **Tertullian, *On the Soul*, 58.8**

528 Every disobedience receives condign punishment, there, nothing is left undestroyed, nothing remitted without penalty, nothing is exempt from the obedience of Christ. **St. Basil, *On the Judgment of God* (*Ascetical Works*, p. 49)**

529 He has introduced the other way—that of punishment and torture, which is very bitter, to be sure, but nevertheless salutary. **St. John Chrysostom, *Commentary on St. John the Apostle and Evangelist*, I.96**

530 If God threatened us without ever intending to fulfill His threat, we should call Him deceitful instead of merciful, and that would be sacrilegious. **St. Gregory the Great, *Dialogues*, 4.46**

531 He condemns those whom He judges worthy of damnation; though they suffer—each one his own evils—He does what is good. **St. Augustine, *Continence*, 6.15**

532 Should we not condemn ourselves to the fire of hell for allowing Him who has given His life for us to waste away in hunger? **St. John Chrysostom, *Commentary on St. John the Apostle and Evangelist*, I.265**

533 Now, there are two kinds of abandonment [by God], for there is one by dispensation which is for our instruction and there is another which is absolute rejection.... Absolute abandonment is when God has done everything for a man's salvation, yet the man of his own accord remains obdurate and uncured, or rather, incorrigible, and is then given over to absolute perdition, like Judas. **St. John of Damascus, *Orthodox Faith*, 2.29**

534 Some [pagan thinkers] rouse such an attraction in us that we could wish to have them freed from the sufferings of Hell—but human feeling is not the same as the justice of the creator. **St. Augustine, *Letters*, 164**

535 The Divine Judgment, remember, is just and awesome.
Theodoret of Cyrus, *Commentary on the Psalms*, 6.8

536 If man made himself deserving of an eternal evil, it was because he drowned within himself a good that could have been eternal.
St. Augustine, *City of God*, 21.12

537 For this reason the groans of the poor go before you, and pale faces follow to accuse you; a throng of wailing parents assails you, so that you may be condemned by the heavenly Judge and have your fill of punishment for having locked yourself out from the abundance of your barns by refusing access to others. **St. Peter Chrysologos, *Sermons*, 3.104.5**

538 I ask, is there anyone rash enough to affirm as a fact that the holy angels, along with holy men who will then be on par with the angels of God, will pray for the damned, both human and angelic, that they be freed by mercy from the sufferings which, in fact, they certainly deserved? This is something which no man of sound faith has ever said. **St. Augustine, *City of God*, 21.24**

539 So too the human being who squanders the gift of nature, the blessing of his soul, the benefit of his reason, the excellence of intelligence, the judgment of his mind, his artistic talent, and his good upbringing, and invests them in unfruitful and empty endeavors, robs his Author of fruit, and is of no use to his Cultivator. Just as the tree deserves to be excised from the earth, so does this person deserve to be excised from life. **St. Peter Chrysologos,** *Sermons,* **3.106.2**

540 But with regard to paying the last farthing, the expression can be quite reasonably understood as the equivalent of saying that nothing is left unpunished. **St. Augustine,** *Commentary on the Lord's Sermon on the Mount,* **1.11.30**

541 What can mercy do for him to whom everything has ended in punishment? Or what help can supplication before his father obtain for him whose accuser has his place in his father's bosom? **St. Peter Chrysologos,** *Sermons,* **3.124.6**

542 Such impious and sinful men as the gospel judges worthy of such punishment shall be consumed by eternal fire. **St. Augustine,** *The Proceedings of Pelagius,* **3.10**

543 Oftentimes a murderer, guilty of fifty murders, is beheaded once; how will he pay the penalty for the forty-nine? If after this world there is no justice and retribution, you charge God with injustice. **St. Cyril of Jerusalem,** *Catechesis,* **18.4**

544 For if it is said, "The wicked shall not rise to be judged," the meaning is that they shall rise, though not to be judged but to be sentenced. For God needs no lengthy scrutiny, but as soon as the wicked rise again, their punishment forthwith follows. **St. Cyril of Jerusalem,** *Catechesis,* **18.14**

545 If you refuse to throw aside your sin you will perish with it, for sin cannot go unpunished. God wants to kill sin, not to strike the sinner.... You, however, love and embrace your sin: that which might have perished without you is going to perish with you. Because you might have received heaven if your sin had perished, by keeping it you will suffer eternal punishment. **St. Caesarius of Arles,** *Sermons,* **17.4–5**

546 Yet, the longer He awaits your amendment, the harsher will be your punishment if you refuse to amend. **St. Caesarius of Arles, *Sermons*, 17.4**

547 The beginning of [God's] retribution comes about when the wicked person, receiving the reward which was required for his error in itself, by a just judgment is allowed to remain in his wickedness; the completion comes when, for these same inequities, he will be tortured by eternal fire. **Fulgentius, *On the Forgiveness of Sins*, 13.1**

548 If you believe on the basis of God's word that the souls of the saints are in heaven, you must also believe that the souls of the wicked are in hell. For, if eternal justice brings God's chosen ones to glory, does it not follow that it also brings the wicked to their doom? **St. Gregory the Great, *Dialogues*, 4.29**

549 God does well by rewarding the evil with destruction, although destruction is an evil for them who now here unjustly deserted and afterwards will be justly tortured. **Fulgentius, *To Monimus*, 1.27.1**

Fear of Hell

550 Lest anyone repeat the ... claim that our statements that sinners are punished in everlasting fire are just boastful words calculated to instill terror, and that we want men to live a virtuous life through fear and not because such a life is pleasant, I will make this brief reply that, if it is not as we say, then there is no God. **St. Justin Martyr, *Second Apology*, 128**

551 You threaten the fire that burns for an hour and in a little while is quenched; for you do not know the fire of future judgment and of eternal punishment, the fire reserved for the wicked. Why do you delay? Come, do as you wish. ***The Martyrdom of St. Polycarp*, 11.1**

552 And the fire of their savage torturers was cool to them, for they kept before their eyes the escape from the eternal and unquenchable fire. *The Martyrdom of St. Polycarp, 2.3*

553 The heat of Hell could effect nothing against His confessors and martyrs. **St. Cyprian,** *Letters,* **6.3**

554 I behold there such wailing and unceasing tears as can never be described by anyone. I behold some making shrill noises with their teeth and leaping with their whole bodies and trembling from head to foot. I throw myself upon the ground and pray to God that I may never endure the trials which are their fate. **Paschasius of Dumium,** *Questions and Answers of the Greek Fathers,* **12**

555 Let him certainly be afraid to die who, not having been reborn of water and the spirit, is delivered up to the fires of Hell. **St. Cyprian,** *Mortality,* **14**

556 To the man who refrains from committing injustice, but is negligent in showing mercy, we say: "Every tree that doth not yield fruit shall be cut down and cast into the fire." **St. Basil,** *On Mercy and Justice* **(Ascetical Works, p. 511)**

557 What profit is there that you find some relief from your pain in this world if you are going to be consigned to eternal fire? **St. John Chrysostom,** *Discourses against Judaizing Christians,* **8.5.6**

558 Why did He threaten the punishment of hell for those who do not listen to His commands? Because, even though we do not obey, He is very much concerned for us, since He is so good. **St. John Chrysostom,** *Commentary on St. John the Apostle and Evangelist,* **1.96**

559 We might say, then, that a vision of hell and its torments is helpful to some, but for others it is the cure of even grander condemnation. Some are forewarned by these visions and turn from evil. Others, on

the contrary, unwilling to avoid hell, even after seeing and considering its torments, become all the more blameworthy. **St. Gregory the Great, *Dialogues*, 4.37**

560 Let us not watch ourselves falling into everlasting punishment through omission and negligence in this short time, but let us be vigilant. **St. John Chrysostom, *Commentary on St. John the Apostle and Evangelist*, 1.119**

561 He who fears Hell does not fear to sin, he fears to burn; but the one who hates sin itself as he hates Hell, he is the one who fears to sin. **St. Augustine, *Letters*, 145**

562 I stand in terror of his left hand, and the goats, and the rebukes levied against them by the one who has summoned them. They are condemned to take their places on the left not because they stole, or committed sacrilege, or fornicated, or violated any other taboo, but because they did not serve Christ through the poor. **St. Gregory of Nazianzus, *Selected Orations*, 14.39**

563 Be enkindled, my brethren, that you may not burn with the fire in which the demons are destined to burn. **St. Augustine, *Sermons of the Liturgical Seasons*, 234.3**

564 If the prison of Tartarus lies under the earth, if there is burning heat, if there is an underworld with unending torment, if there is a grim attendant to drag us away to these punishments after our labors in this world, why are we surprised? ... Why do we not have as our only concern to despise all else and to escape from such evils, lest by living for this world and by being concerned about other matters we suddenly be dragged away to suffer such enormously terrible and cruel punishments? **St. Peter Chrysologos, *Sermons*, 3.124.9**

565 The long-suffering patience of a merciful God causes many seamless and faithless unbelievers to sin with temerity, thinking that God is not an avenger of sin because He does not choose to punish sinners immediately. **St. Augustine, *The Christian Life*, 2**

566 We shall all rise again, but we shall not all rejoice. **St. Augustine, *Sermons of the Liturgical Seasons*, 235.3**

Deliverance from Hell

567 No one, in truth, will rescue you from hell except the assistance which you obtain from the poor. **St. John Chrysostom, *Commentary on St. John the Apostle and Evangelist*, 1.267**

568 Only the quality of good works directed towards the destitute would determine the sentence for the ungodly to burn with the devil. **St Leo the Great, *Sermons*, 11.1**

569 Since capital crimes—that is, murder, adultery, theft, and bearing false witness—not only throw men out of heaven but even cast them into hell, let us repair the rest of our daily sins, which are never lacking, by constant almsgiving and forgiveness of our enemies. **St. Caesarius of Arles, *Sermons*, 19.2**

570 Therefore, let him stretch forth his hands to give alms, in order that he may be able to escape eternal hell-fire. **St. Caesarius of Arles, *Sermons*, 27.2**

571 Anyone, therefore, who wants to escape eternal punishment should be baptized and justified in Christ, and so pass sincerely from Satan to Christ. **St. Augustine, *City of God*, 21.16**

572 Another view of freedom from eternal punishment is that of those who do not extend the promise of impunity to all men, but only to those who, by reason of baptism, are members of the Body of Christ. **St. Augustine, *City of God*, 21.18**

573 Still another view promises impunity, not to all baptized Christians and partakers of Holy Communion, but only to Catholics, and this irrespective of the evil of their lives.   **St. Augustine, *City of God*, 21.19**

574 The fact is that there is no way of waving or weakening the words which the Lord has told us that He will pronounce in the last judgment: "Depart from me, you accursed ones, into the everlasting fire in which the devil and his angels are to burn."   **St. Augustine, *City of God*, 21.23**

575 Dead men have their sins still clinging to them, unless before their demise they purged them away through the intercession of their tears before God. Hell, armed with due punishments, awaits its prisoner. **St. Valerian, *Homilies*, 1.3**

576 Whoever commits theft, or does not fear to commit adultery, bear false witness, curse, or commit perjury, whether men or women, receive the name of Christian and the sacrament of baptism, not as remedy but to their own judgment. Unless these people do penance, they will perish forever.   **St. Caesarius of Arles, *Sermons*, 16.3**

577 Grant me a little time that I may repent for my sins, for in hell no one has the power to confess his sins.   **St. Jerome, *Homilies*, 30**

The Road to Hell

578 Perhaps some wonder why the Evangelist calls the way of death wide and easy to travel, since the journey through life is hard at every step. But, who ever found the descent to a lower level hard?   **St. Valerian, *Homilies*, 2.1**

579 Thus it comes about that the gate of death receives many men, for a man arrives more easily when he travels without any check.   **St. Valerian, *Homilies*, 2.5**

580 This, in my opinion, is the gulf, which is not an earthly abyss, that the judgment between the two opposite choices of life creates. One has chosen the pleasure of this life and has not remedied this bad choice by a change of heart; he produces for himself a place devoid of good hereafter, digging this unavoidable necessity for himself like some deep and trackless pit. **St. Gregory of Nyssa, *On the Soul and the Resurrection* (*Ascetical Works*, p.234)**

581 If the devil finds any souls careless and imprudent, he fixes on them again with traps more ruthless still and brings them, snatched from the Church's paradise, into the company of his damnation.
St. Leo the Great, *Sermons*, 70.4

582 Although they themselves were mad, they believed that they were sane and did not hope for the retribution of divine justice and thus did not make any effort to reform their lives. They delighted to live licentiously here below for a few short days and did not believe that after a little while they would be tortured with eternal punishments.
Fulgentius, *On the Forgiveness of Sins*, 3.2

583 What is a man when he does not restrain his unlawful desires with the reason given to him, except an irrational sheep? Of these men it is said: "Man, for all his splendor, does not abide; he resembles the beasts that perish." What follows such a man, except an eternal death of torments? **St. Caesarius of Arles, *Sermons*, 100A.6**

584 Envy has always been the killer of its own.... The one who welcomes it endures his own unending punishments, because he is chasing to have his personal torturer always inside himself. **St. Peter Chrysologos, *Sermons*, 3.172.2**

585 Have you already forgotten ... what He will say to those who have not given alms: "Cast them into the eternal fire"? **St. Augustine, *Sermons of the Liturgical Seasons*, 198.2**

586 Those who go into fire and are burned are the ones into whose hearts repentance no longer enters, because of their unbridled lust and the impious acts they put into execution. **The Shepherd of Hermas, Visions, 7.2**

587 If man made himself deserving of eternal evil, it was because he drowned within himself a good which could have been eternal.
St. Augustine, City of God, 21.12

588 Am I not permitted to do what I wish in my own house? I answer: "You are not so permitted. They who act thus go to hell and will burn in everlasting fire." **St. Augustine, Sermons of the Liturgical Seasons, 224.3**

589 Laziness throws us down even from heaven, while discouragement hurls us down even to the very abyss. **St. John Chrysostom, On Repentance and Almsgiving, 1.15**

590 Indeed, nothing so estranges from the mercy of God and gives over to the fire of hell as the tyranny of pride. **St. John Chrysostom, Commentary on St. John the Apostle and Evangelist, 1.94**

591 He who, to keep or gain those things [of this world], will commit murder, adultery, fornication, idolatry, and anything else of this sort will not be saved through fire because of his foundation [of faith], but, having lost the foundation, he will be tormented by eternal fire.
St. Augustine, Eight Questions of Dulcitius, Question 1

592 If we depart from here uninitiated, even if we have earthly blessings without number, nothing else will welcome us than hell, and the poisonous serpent, and unquenchable fire, and indissoluble bonds.
St. John Chrysostom, Commentary on St. John the Apostle and Evangelist, 1.249

593 The presumptuous one, too, stands at the steps of death, since, by debating, he has stripped off his faith. **St. Ephrem the Syrian, The Hymns of Faith, 23.2**

594 Even if you were burned alive for the name of Christ, you would suffer the punishment of eternal torment if you persisted in remaining outside the Church. **St. Augustine, *Letters*, 173**

Those Condemned

595 They who do not walk to God in justice are handed over to the devil. **St. Jerome, *Homilies*, 34**

596 But those who have been unbelievers or have not been baptized or, even though baptized, have after their baptism returned to their idols and homicide and adultery and perjury and other wicked ways and who died without repentance; all who have been found such shall be condemned with the devil and with all the demons whom they worshiped and whose works they performed and shall be sent in the flesh to eternal fire in hell, where that inexhaustible fire lives forever, and that flesh now recovered at the resurrection suffers eternal torments and groaning. **Martin of Braga, *Reforming the Rustics*, 14**

597 If a man disdains the divine will, he can only use his own to his own destruction. **St. Augustine, *City of God*, 13.21**

598 What one refuses to give to the poor he gives to the moths, and with his clothes he is a devourer of the body, as the Lord says: "Their worms will never die." The poor person's hunger has struck Christ, the pain of the human being has pierced God's heart ... and contempt for the destitute has such far-reaching effects as to have hurt the Creator. **St. Peter Chrysologos, *Sermons*, 3.137.9**

599 If arrogance dominates a man, what is left for him save the sentence of damnation? **St. Valerian, *Homilies*, 14.3**

600 Divine justice permitted evil not to be beyond the limits of order, and has brought it back and confined it to an order befitting it. **St. Augustine, *Divine Providence and the Problem of Evil*, 1.7.23**

601 Whoever has not been humane, devoted, gracious, kind, and gentle cannot escape the fire of hell. **St. Augustine, *The Christian Life*, 10**

602 Thus, when the innocent will rise up, terror and death will gain possession of the unjust and the unholy. **St. Peter Chrysologos, *Sermons*, 3.77.9**

603 He hates all who work inequity but, in addition, He destroys all who tell lies. **St. Augustine, *Lying*, 6**

604 But a frightful punishment hangs over those [who think their deceitful language goes unpunished], and penalty, judgment, and every sort of torture, and fire unquenchable awaits them. **St. Cyril of Alexandria, *Festal Letters*, 9.5**

605 Just as the one who blasphemes the Spirit is without forgiveness both in the present age and in the future, so too has this one who has inflicted an insult on the Wisdom of God completely bypassed judgment and fully descended to punishment. **St. Peter Chrysologos, *Sermons*, 3.177.7**

606 God's sentence of damnation will be pronounced on the wicked, both angels and men; can we suppose it will hold for demons but not for men? Only if men's imaginings have more weight than God's words! **St. Augustine, *City of God*, 21.23**

607 The debtor must be punished who neglects to pay back his obligation when love is all that is required. **St. Peter Chrysologos, *Sermons*, 3.94.5**

608 Such a man, for becoming contaminated [with bad doctrine], will depart into unquenchable fire; and so will anyone who listens to him. **St. Ignatius of Antioch, *Letter to the Ephesians*, 16**

609 Do you hear how violent and implacable is the punishment he assigns to those who decide to practice a secret impiety? **St. Cyril of Alexandria, *Festal Letters*, 9.5**

610 But as a consequence of their own deeds, for those who practice evil there will be wrath and fury, affliction and anguish, in accordance with what they have treasured up for themselves. **Origen, *Commentary on the Epistle to the Romans*, 2.6.1**

611 Pagans and sinners, the dry trees you see, will be found to be dry and fruitless in that world. They will be burned as firewood and will be manifest, because their activity own life was wicked. **The Shepherd of Hermas, *Parables*, Fourth Parable, 4**

612 Sinners will be burned, because they sinned without repenting; pagans because they did not know their Creator. **The Shepherd of Hermas, *Parables*, Fourth Parable, 4**

613 Our Lord Jesus Christ does not absolve from punishment even sins committed in ignorance. **St. Basil, *On the Judgement of God* (*Ascetical Works*, p. 47)**

614 It is necessary merely to mention those who are to stand at the left hand of Our Lord Jesus Christ on the great and terrible day of judgement; those to whom He ... will say: "Depart from me, you cursed, into everlasting fire which was prepared for the devil." **St. Basil, *On the Judgement of God* (*Ascetical Works*, p. 53)**

615 Will, perhaps, they who did not perform works of mercy enter into everlasting fire, and will they not enter into it who stole another's goods, or who, by injuring the temple of God in themselves, were unmerciful to themselves, as if works of mercy were any profit without charity? **St. Augustine, *Eight Questions of Dulcitius*, Question 1**

616 At the same time God will say to those on His left: "Depart ... into the everlasting fire which was prepared for the devil and his angels." It is a dreadful sentence; a fearful sentence! **St. Augustine, *Sermons of the Liturgical Seasons*, 265.2**

617 Since "those on the left" have nothing to do with "those on the right," they will—by sentence of the Almighty Judge—be cast into the fire devised for tormenting "the devil and his angels"—to have partnership in punishment with the one whom they chose to follow. **St. Leo the Great, *Sermons*, 9.2.1**

618 And so it will happen that punishment will be accorded to those who are confounded, and reward to those who have been faithful. **St. Augustine, *Sermons of the Liturgical Seasons*, 198.2**

619 They are condemned, not because they did evil, but because they did not do good. **St. Augustine, *The Christian Life*, 10**

620 Because evil-doers delight in their evil, that is in their dark deeds, and the punishment of torture is to follow them, when the Lord says "exterior darkness," He adds also: "There shall be weeping and gnashing of teeth," lest the wicked should madly think to have in that torture such pleasures as they have here. **St. Augustine, *Letters*, 140.23**

621 They had sought mercy too late, when the time of judgment was at hand.... It is right for them to be answered, "Amen, I say to you, I know you not," although, doubtless, He that says it knows everything; but this "I know you not" is the same as "You know me not when you choose to trust in yourselves rather than in me." **St. Augustine, *Letters*, 144.35**

622 But those, to whom is transferred the role of the Egyptians [in Exodus], the power having been permitted them temporarily by the authority of God, showing their anger will persecute the Christians with the most serious tortures; yet all those same enemies of Christ with their king, Antichrist, being caught in the lake of eternal fire, which because of the great darkness that intervenes, is entered upon while it is not seen, will receive the lot of perpetual damnation to burn with everlasting torments. **Paulus Orosius, *Seven Books of History against the Pagans*, 7.27**

The Fires of Hell

623 The Son of Man will send forth his angels, and they will gather out of his kingdom all scandals and those who work iniquity, and cast them into the furnace of fire, where there will be weeping and gnashing of teeth. **St. Augustine, *City of God*, 20.5**

624 So after the cultivation that occurs in the era of the gospel, the ax of the Last Judgment will cut down the trees that have not borne fruit, and the final conflagration will take them and burn them to ashes.
St. Peter Chrysologos, *Sermons*, 3.106.7

625 Therefore, we ought above all to ponder chiefly those punishments in which the man lives with uninterrupted pain, where torments never fail to afflict his body and the arms of the torturer never weary. We can easily avoid all these afflictions if we hold fast to the reins of discipline. **St. Valerian, *Homilies*, 1.3**

626 I behold an immeasurable sea of boiling fire, and men weeping and wailing, and the flood of that fire, as some think, reaches the heavens; and in that tremendous sea are innumerable men thrown down from earth; all the shrubbery is burned like dry wood, and the mercy of the Lord is turned away from them because of their injustices.
Paschasius of Dumium, *Questions and Answers of the Greek Fathers*, 12

627 O goods of the world which are evil in hell! Fire came to serve the rich man, and torturers to obey him in his cruelty. He endures the harsh attendants of hell. He is tormented and shouts: O just and innocent judge, these punishments are now balanced against my sins!
St. Caesarius of Arles, *Sermons*, 31.4

628 There are some who think that both the "fire" and the "worm" here mentioned are meant as pains of the soul rather than of the body.... However, those who have no doubt that in hell there will be sufferings both for soul and body hold that the body will be burned in fire while the soul will be gnawed, as it were, by the "worm" of grief. **St. Augustine, *City of God*, 21.9**

629 Wherefore, the unquenchable fire and everlasting torment have been prepared for the Devil and his evil spirits and for them who follow him. **St. John of Damascus, *Orthodox Faith*, 2.4**

630 The one thing which we may by no means believe is that bodies in hell will be such that they will be unaffected by any pains inflicted by fire. **St. Augustine, *City of God*, 21.9**

631 When the body is in such pain, the body must be tortured by fruitless repentance. **St. Augustine, *City of God*, 21.9**

632 In the weeping of the eyes and the gnashing of the teeth, he shows through the metaphor of the bodily members the magnitude of the torments. **St. Jerome, *Commentary on Matthew*, 3.22.13**

633 If these incorporeal beings, the Devil and his angels, are going to be tortured by physical fire, is it incredible that souls should be able to suffer physical torments even before they are again untied with the body? **St. Gregory the Great, *Dialogues*, 4.30**

634 If the incorporeal spirit can be held in the body to which it gives life, why should it not be held for punishment in a place where it endures punishment? **St. Gregory the Great, *Dialogues*, 4.30**

635 One and the same fire will serve as punishment for both men and devils, as we see from the words of Christ: "Depart from me, accursed ones, into the everlasting fire which was prepared for the devil and his angels." **St. Augustine, *City of God*, 21.10**

636 What is certain is that both men and devils will suffer, as the Truth has told us, in the same fire. **St. Augustine, *City of God*, 21.10**

637 When we say that the spirit is held by fire we mean that it is in torment of fire by seeing and feeling. Seeing the fire, it begins to suffer, and when it sees itself attached by flames it feel the burning. In this way a corporeal substance burns an incorporeal one, because an invisible burn and an invisible pain are received from visible fire. **St. Gregory the Great, *Dialogues*, 4.30**

638 [The rich man says] I am tied with the fetters of my sins, so that I cannot escape. Minute by minute I am pricked so that I feel pain. The fire rages in me, yet spares me; it tortures but preserves me; it does not punish all of me, but is cruel when it does not. **St. Caesarius of Arles, *Sermons*, 31.4**

639 Since Christ describes the condemned sinner Dives surrounded by the flames of hell, no one with understanding would deny that the souls of the wicked are held fast in fire. **St. Gregory the Great, *Dialogues*, 4.30**

640 Exterior darkness can be understood as corporeal pains—since the body is exterior to the soul. **St. Augustine, *Letters*, 144.23**

Greater and Lesser Suffering

641 If anyone thinks that there will not be different penalties, let him read what is written: "It will be more tolerable for Sodom in the day of judgment than for that city." **St. Augustine, *Letters*, 184A**

642 There is one kind of fire in hell, but it does not torment all sinners in the same way, for each one feels its torments according to the degree of guilt. Just as in this world many live under the one sun, yet not all feel the heat of the sun to the same degree—some feel it more, others less—so in hell there are many degrees of burning in the one fire. There is no need of different types of fire to produce different types of burning, either in this world under the one sun or in hell in the torments of one fire. **St. Gregory the Great, *Dialogues*, 4.45**

643   As for the eternal fire, this will undoubtedly affect people different-ly according to their deserts and the pain will be made slight or serious either by varying the degree of intensity of the fire itself, according to the guilt of the sufferers, or by varying the sensitivity of the sinners to a hell that is the same for all.   **St. Augustine,** *City of God,* **21.17**

644   If I am a sinner, will I suffer the same punishment if I have offended just once, as I will if I sin twice or a third time and even more frequently? Not at all. The amount of punishment is to be measured according to the manner, number, and measure of sin for God will give us "the bread of tears and tears to drink," but "with ample measure." Every man will reap the things he sought in this life by sinning, more or less.   **St. Caesarius of Arles,** *Sermons,* **108.4**

645   Do not be surprised that … those who are "medium sinners" have been thrown into the lake of fire with the Devil and the Antichrist. For a different punishment is meant there, just as there is a different kind of fiery heat: one is a sort of continuous burning heat, the other is less so and mild, even though both are called fiery heat.   **Oecumenius,** *Commentary on the Apocalypse,* **11.9**

646   The most that can be said is that the pains suffered may be lighter and milder than the wickedness deserved. In this way the anger of God will endure, yet in His anger He will not shut up His mercies. **St. Augustine,** *City of God,* **21.24**

647   Heretics and schismatics who are separated from this Body can, indeed, receive the sacrament, but to no avail—in fact to their harm— since the result is to increase the pain rather than to curtail the length of their punishment.   **St. Augustine,** *City of God,* **21.25**

648   Whence also is that rich sinner who … is burning in the fires of the consuming flames; among all the parts of his body, his mouth and tongue especially pay the penalty because, perchance he sinned more by his tongue and by his mouth.   **St. Cyprian,** *Letters,* **59.3**

649 It behooves us to understand what sufferings they will endure who join avarice to their other sins. Though devoid of all other sins, they whom the crime of avarice alone has condemned to death are to be afflicted with the greatest punishment. **Salvian the Presbyter, *The Four Books of the Church*, 2.12**

Longing for Heaven and the Father

650 You would therefore have to remain outside, and lumbered with these burdens [of sin] to repent all too late, already contemplating before your eyes the punishments prepared for you, that terrible fire that is not extinguished and the worm that does not die. **St. John Chrysostom, *Homilies on Genesis*, 22.21**

651 [For the rich man in hell] his whole being was in anguish; his eyes alone were free, free to gaze on the happiness of the other man. He was allowed the liberty of his eyes to be tortured the more because he does not enjoy what the other has. **St. Jerome, *Homilies*, 86**

652 He still calls a son the one whom he sees is a vassal of hell, an offspring of punishments, by now the lowest slave in Gehenna. But he calls him a son, in order that his son's lack of pity become clearer and clearer, since the pity manifested in the father's words perdures even towards such as him. **St. Peter Chrysologos, *Sermons*, 3.123.2**

653 [God says] I call you a son, so that you may understand that what you are suffering is the result of your sentence and not of wrath. I call you a son, in order for my patience to last for me and your punishment to last for you. **St. Peter Chrysologos, *Sermons*, 3.123.2**

654 Yet there is another reason why they burn, namely, that the elect may see in God all the joys they experience, and may see in the damned all the tortures they escaped. **St. Gregory the Great, *Dialogues*, 4.46**

The Second Death

655 They really did perish for whom, as they leave this world, the punishment and pain of a greater judgment are waiting. **St. Augustine, The Christian Life, 5**

656 There can be no greater or worse death than where death itself never dies. **St. Augustine, City of God, 6.12**

657 There is also a total death for man, a death of body and soul, namely when a soul, abandoned by God, abandons the body. This is the second death which the Savior meant when He said: "Fear him who is able to destroy both body and soul in hell." **St. Augustine, City of God, 13.2**

658 It is true that, when a man is finally damned, he does not lose sensation; nevertheless, because his feelings are not gentle enough to give pleasure nor soothing enough to be restful, but are purifying to the point of pain, they can more properly be called death rather than life. **St. Augustine, City of God, 13.2**

659 The doom in store for those who are not of the City of God is an unending wretchedness that is called "the second death," because neither the soul, cut off from the life of God, nor the body, pounded by perpetual pain, can there be said to live at all. **St. Augustine, City of God, 19.28**

660 And what will make that second death so hard to bear is that there will be no death to end it. **St. Augustine, City of God, 19.28**

The Eternity of Hell

661 Anyone who says that their punishment, which the Lord has said is eternal, can come to an end, shares in the abominable opinion of Origen. **St. Augustine, The Proceedings of Pelagius, 3.10**

662 A man is tortured then, for as many years as there were days of self-indulgence. So you see that, though the period of self-indulgence and deceit is very short, the period of punishment and torture is protracted. **The Shepherd of Hermas, *Parables*, Sixth Parable, 4.2**

663 It does not follow that everything that is eternal is, therefore, blessed—for the pain of Hell is called eternal. **St. Augustine, *City of God*, 11.11**

664 It seems harder to believe that the bodies of the damned are to remain in endless torment than to believe that the bodies of the saints are to continue without pain in everlasting felicity. **St. Augustine, *City of God*, 21.1**

665 It is not easy to find a proof that will convince unbelievers of the possibility of human bodies remaining not merely active, alive, and uncorrupted after death, but also of continuing forever in the torments of fire. **St. Augustine, *City of God*, 21.2**

666 One thing that will happen, and most certainly happen, is what God, through His Prophet, said concerning the punishment of hell being eternal: "There worm shall not die, and there fire shall not be quenched." **St. Augustine, *City of God*, 21.9**

667 The term imposed by the judge is never measured by the time it took to deserve the penalty. **St. Augustine, *City of God*, 21.11**

668 The reason why eternal punishment seems so hard and unjust to human feeling is that, in the present weakness of our mortal understanding, we lack vision of that lofty and unclouded Wisdom which alone can make it possible for us to understand the enormity that was committed in man's first prevarication. **St. Augustine, *City of God*, 21.12**

669 Hell, where they are shut in, and whence there is no departure. Truly, from that fortress no other except the Lord comes out victorious. **St. Jerome, *Homilies*, 34**

670 Origen was so moved by pity as to think that even the devil and his angels, after very severe and long-continued pains in proportion to their guilt, would be snatched from the flames to join the company of the holy angels. But Origen has rightly been reproved by the Church on more than one account. **St. Augustine, *City of God*, 21.17**

671 It is from Scripture that we know that … they will be received into "everlasting" fire, there to be tortured "forever and ever." **St. Augustine, *City of God*, 21.23**

672 That city is fortified against exit, but it is always open for entrance. **St. Jerome, *Homilies*, 34**

673 No one descends into hell in triumph save You alone, Lord. **St. Jerome, *Homilies*, 34**

674 What kind of imagining is this, to take eternal punishment to mean long-continued punishment and, at the same time, to believe that eternal life is endless, seeing that Christ spoke of both as eternal in the same place and in one and the same sentence? **St. Augustine, *City of God*, 21.23**

675 Therefore, since the eternal life of the saints is to be endless, there can be no doubt that eternal punishment for those who are to endure it will have no end. **St. Augustine, *City of God*, 21.23**

676 It would be an excess of presumption to say in regard to any of these whom God has condemned to everlasting punishment that their punishment would not be everlasting. The effect of such presumption would be either despair or doubt in regard the eternity of everlasting life. **St. Augustine, *City of God*, 21.24**

677 There are some men whom the temporary punishment of this world does fail to overtake, but the insatiable pain of everlasting torment pursues them forever. **St. Valerian, *Homilies*, 1.3**

678 What is the wrath to come? It is that which has no end, which does not release the human being by death, but keeps him enchained, and no longer allows him to have any hope for pardon, once it has condemned him to the penal realm of Tartarus. **St. Peter Chrysologos, Sermons, 3.137.8**

679 In the future time, there is to be no conversion for the wicked, and the penance of such people will be endless as well as useless. Just as forgiveness will never be given to them, so their penance will never be ended. **Fulgentius, *On the Forgiveness of Sins*, 17.3**

Ending

680 When death has closed these eyes, and cold I lie,
   When vision clear my naked spirit enjoys,
   Let it not see one of those deamon faces fierce,
   Relentless, grim, with threatening look and voice,
   Prepared to drag me, stained with many sins,
   Headlong into black yawing caves below,
   There to exact from me all that is due,
   To the last farthing, for my wasted life.

   Aurelius Prudentius Clemens, *The Origin of Sin*, 944–51

BIBLIOGRAPHY

All titles in The Fathers of the Church (FOTC) series are published by the Catholic University of America Press, Washington, D.C.

Ambrose of Milan. *Hexameron, Paradise, and Cain and Abel*. Translated by John J. Savage. FOTC 42. 1961.
———. *Letters*. Translated by Mary Melchior Beyenka, OP. Edited by Roy J. Deferrari. FOTC 26. 1954.
———. *Seven Exegetical Works*. Translated by Michael P. McHugh. Edited by Bernard M. Peebles. FOTC 65. 1972.
———. *Theological and Dogmatic Works*. Translated by Roy J. Deferrari. Edited by Roy J. Deferrari. FOTC 44. 1963.
Andrew of Caesarea. *Commentary on the Apocalypse*. Translated by Eugenia Scarvelis Constantinou. Edited by David G. Hunter. FOTC 123. 2011.
Apostolic Fathers. *The Apostolic Fathers*. Translated by Francis X. Glimm, Joseph M.-F. Marique, SJ, and Gerald G. Walsh, SJ. FOTC 1. 1947.
Augustine of Hippo. *Against Julian*. Translated by Matthew A. Schumacher. Edited by Hermigild Dressler. FOTC 35. 1957.
———. *Christian Instruction; Admonition and Grace; The Christian Combat; Faith, Hope and Charity*. Translated by John J. Gavigan, John Courtney Murray, Robert P. Russell, and Bernard M. Peebles. Edited by Roy J. Deferrari. 2nd ed. FOTC 2. 1950.
———. *Commentary on the Lord's Sermon on the Mount with Seventeen Related Sermons*. Translated by Denis J. Kavanagh. Edited by Hermigild Dressler. FOTC 11. 1951.
———. *Confessions*. Translated by Vernon J. Bourke. Edited by Roy J. Deferrari. FOTC 21. 1953.
———. *Eighty-Three Different Questions*. Translated by David L. Mosher. Edited by Hermigild Dressler. FOTC 70. 1982.

———. *Four Anti-Pelagian Writings.* Translated by John A. Mourant and William J. Collinge. Edited by Thomas P. Halton. FOTC 86. 1992.

———. *Letters (1–82).* Translated by Sr. Wilfrid Parsons, SND. FOTC 12. 1951.

———. *Letters (83–130).* Translated by Sr. Wilfrid Parsons, SND. Edited by Roy J. Deferrari. Translated by FOTC 18. 1953.

———. *Letters (131–64).* Translated by Sr. Wilfrid Parsons, SND. Edited by Roy J. Deferrari. FOTC 20. 1953.

———. *Letters (165–203).* Translated by Sr. Wilfrid Parsons, SND. Edited by Hermigild Dressler. FOTC 30. 1955.

———. *Letters (204–70).* Translated by Sr. Wilfrid Parsons, SND. Edited by Hermigild Dressler. FOTC 32. 1956.

———. *Letters (1*–29*).* Translated by Robert B. Eno, SS. Edited by Thomas P. Halton. FOTC 81. 1989.

———. *On Genesis: Two Books on Genesis against the Manichees; And, on the Literal Interpretation of Genesis: An Unfinished Book.* Translated by Roland J. Teske. Edited by Thomas P. Halton. FOTC 84. 1991.

———. *Sermons on the Liturgical Seasons.* Translated by Mary Sarah Muldowney. Edited by Hermigild Dressler. FOTC 38. 1959.

———. *The Catholic and Manichaean Ways of Life.* Translated by Donald A. Gallagher and Idella J. Gallagher. Edited by Roy J. Deferrari. FOTC 56. 1966.

———. *The City of God, Books I–VII.* Translated by Demetrius B. Zema and Gerald G. Walsh. Edited by Hermigild Dressler. FOTC 8. 1950.

———. *The City of God, Books VIII–XVI.* Translated by Gerald G. Walsh, SJ, and Grace Monahan. Edited by Hermigild Dressler. FOTC 14. 1952.

———. *The City of God, Books XVII–XXII.* Translated by Gerald G. Walsh, SJ, and Daniel J. Honan. Edited by Hermigild Dressler. FOTC 24. 1954.

———. *The Happy Life and Answer to Skeptics and Divine Providence and the Problem of Evil and Soliloquies.* Translated by Denis J. Kavanagh, Robert P. Russell, Thomas F. Gilligan, and Ludwig Schopp. Edited by Ludwig Schopp. FOTC 5. 1948.

———. *The Immortality of the Soul; The Magnitude of the Soul; On Music; The Advantage of Believing; On Faith in Things Unseen.* Translated by Ludwig Schopp, John J. McMahon, Robert Catesby Taliaferro, Luanne Meagher, Roy J. Deferrari, and Mary Francis McDonald. Edited by Hermigild Dressler. FOTC 4. 1947.

———. *The Retractations.* Translated by Mary Inez Bogan, RSM. Edited by Roy J. Deferrari. FOTC 60. 1968.

———. *The Teacher; The Free Choice of the Will; Grace and Free Will.* Translated by Robert P. Russell. Edited by Roy J. Deferrari. FOTC 59. 1968.

———. *The Trinity.* Translated by Stephen McKenna. Edited by Hermigild Dressler. FOTC 45. 1963.

———. *Tractates on the Gospel of John 1–10.* Translated by John W. Rettig. Edited by Thomas P. Halton. FOTC 78. 1988.

————. *Tractates on the Gospel of John 11–27.* Translated by John W. Rettig. Edited by Thomas P. Halton. FOTC 79. 1988.

————. *Tractates on the Gospel of John 28–54.* Translated by John W. Rettig. Edited by Thomas P. Halton. FOTC 88. 1993.

————. *Tractates on the Gospel of John 55–111.* Translated by John W. Rettig. Edited by Thomas P. Halton. FOTC 90. 1994.

————. *Tractates on the Gospel of John, 112–24; Tractates on the First Epistle of John.* Translated by John W. Rettig. Edited by Thomas P. Halton. FOTC 92. 1995.

————. *Treatises on Marriage and Other Subjects.* Translated by Charles T. Wilcox, Charles T. Huegelmeyer, John McQuade, Marie Liguori, Robert P. Russell, John A. Lacy, and Ruth Wentworth Brown. Edited by Roy J. Deferrari. FOTC 27. 1955.

————. *Treatises on Various Subjects.* Translated by Mary Sarah Muldowney, Harold B. Jaffee, Mary Francis McDonald, Luanne Meagher, M. Clement Eagan, and Mary E. DeFerrari. Edited by Roy J. Deferrari and Hermigild Dressler. FOTC 16. 1952.

Barsanuphius and John. *Barsanuphius and John: Letters.* Translated by John Chryssavgis. Edited by Thomas P. Halton. FOTC 113. 2006.

————. *Barsanuphius and John: Letters.* Translated by John Chryssavgis. Edited by Thomas P. Halton. FOTC 114. 2007.

Basil of Caesarea. *Against Eunomius.* Translated by Mark DelCogliano and Andrew Radde-Gallwitz. FOTC 122. 2011.

————. *Ascetical Works.* Translated by M. Monica Wagner. Edited by Roy J. Deferrari. FOTC 9. 1962.

————. *Exegetic Homilies.* Translated by Sr. Agnes Clare Way, CDP. FOTC 46. 1963.

————. *Letters (1–185).* Translated by Sr. Agnes Clare Way, CDP. Edited by Hermigild Dressler. FOTC 13. 1951.

————. *Letters (186–368).* Translated by Sr. Agnes Clare Way, CDP. Edited by Roy J. Deferrari. FOTC 28. 1955.

Braulio of Saragossa and Fructuosus of Braga. *Iberian Fathers.* Vol. 2. Translated by Claude W. Barlow. Edited by Roy J. Deferrari. FOTC 63. 1969.

Caesarius of Arles. *Sermons (1–80).* Translated by Sr. Mary Magdeleine Mueller, OSF. Edited by Hermigild Dressler and Bernard M. Peebles. FOTC 31. 1956.

————. *Sermons (81–186).* Translated by Sr. Mary Magdeleine Mueller, OSF. Edited by Hermigild Dressler and Bernard M. Peebles. FOTC 47. 1964.

————. *Sermons (187–238).* Translated by Sr. Mary Magdeleine Mueller, OSF. Edited by Hermigild Dressler and Bernard M. Peebles. FOTC 66. 1973.

Clement of Alexandria. *Christ the Educator.* Translated by P. Simon Wood. FOTC 23. 1954.

————. *Stromateis, Books One to Three.* Translated by John Ferguson. Edited by Thomas P. Halton. FOTC 85. 1991.

Cyril of Alexandria. *Commentary on the Twelve Prophets.* Translated by Robert C. Hill. Edited by Thomas P. Halton. FOTC 115. 2007.

————. *Commentary on the Twelve Prophets.* Translated by Robert C. Hill. Edited by Thomas P. Halton. FOTC 116. 2008.

————. *Commentary on the Twelve Prophets.* Translated by Robert C. Hill. Edited by David G. Hunter. FOTC 124. 2012.

————. *Festal Letters, 1–12.* Translated by Philip R. Amidon. Edited by John J. O'Keefe. FOTC 118. 2009.

————. *Festal Letters, 13–30.* Translated by Philip R. Amidon. Edited by John J. O'Keefe and David G. Hunter. FOTC 127. 2013.

————. *Letters, 1–50.* Translated by John I. McEnerney. Edited by Thomas P. Halton. FOTC 76. 1987.

————. *Letters, 51–110.* Translated by John I. McEnerney. Edited by Thomas P. Halton. FOTC 77. 1987.

————. *Three Christological Treatises.* Translated by Daniel King. FOTC 129. 2014.

Cyril of Jerusalem. *The Works of Saint Cyril of Jerusalem.* Vol. 1. Translated by Leo P. McCauley and Anthony A. Stephenson. Edited by Roy J. Deferrari. FOTC 61. 1969.

————. *The Works of Saint Cyril of Jerusalem.* Vol. 2. Translated by Leo P. McCauley and Anthony A. Stephenson. Edited by Bernard M. Peebles. FOTC 64. 1970.

Cyprian of Carthage. *Letters (1–81).* Translated by Rose Bernard Donna. Edited by Hermigild Dressler. FOTC 51. 1964.

————. *Treatises.* Edited and translated by Roy J. Deferrari. FOTC 36. 1958.

Didymus the Blind. *Commentary on Zechariah.* Translated by Robert C. Hill. Edited by Thomas P. Halton. FOTC 111. 2006.

Ephrem the Syrian. *The Hymns on Faith.* Translated by Jeffrey T. Wickes. FOTC 130. 2015.

————. *Selected Prose Works.* Translated by Edward G. Mathews Jr. and Joseph P. Amar. Edited by Thomas P. Halton and Kathleen McVey. FOTC 91. 2004.

Epiphanius of Cyprus. *Ancoratus.* Translated by Young Richard Kim. FOTC 128. 2014.

Eugippius. *The Life of Saint Severin.* Translated by Ludwig Bieler and Ludmilla Krestan. Edited by Roy J. Deferrari. FOTC 55. 1965.

Eusebius of Caesarea. *Ecclesiastical History, Books 1–5.* Edited and translated by Roy J. Deferrari. FOTC 19. 1953.

————. *Ecclesiastical History, Books 6–10.* Translated by Roy J. Deferrari. FOTC 29. 1955.

Fulgentius. *Fulgentius: Selected Works.* Translated by Robert B. Eno, SS. Edited by Thomas P. Halton. FOTC 95. 1997.

Fulgentius and Scythian Monks. *Fulgentius of Ruspe and the Scythian Monks: Correspondence on Christology and Grace.* Translated by Rob Roy McGregor and Donald Fairbairn. FOTC 126. 2013.

Gregory the Great. *Dialogues.* Translated by Odo John Zimmerman. Edited by Hermigild Dressler. FOTC 39. 1959.

Gregory Nazianzen and Ambrose of Milan. *Funeral Orations.* Translated by Leo P.

McCauley, John J. Sullivan, Martin R. P. McGuire, and Roy J. Deferrari. FOTC 22. 1953.

Gregory Nazianzen. *Select Orations*. Translated by Martha Vinson. Edited by Thomas P. Halton. FOTC 107. 2003.

———. *Three Poems: Concerning His Own Affairs, Concerning Himself and the Bishops, Concerning His Own Life*. Translated by Denis Molaise Meehan. Edited by Thomas P. Halton. FOTC 75. 1987.

Gregory of Nyssa. *Anti-Apollinarian Writings*. Translated by Robin Orton. Edited by David G. Hunter. FOTC 131. 2015.

———. *Ascetical Works*. Translated by Virginia Woods Callahan. FOTC 58. 1967.

Gregory Thaumaturgus. *Life and Works*. Translated by Michael Slusser. Edited by Thomas P. Halton. FOTC 98. 1998.

Hilary of Poitiers. *Commentary on Matthew*. Translated by D. H. Williams. Edited by David G. Hunter. FOTC 125. 2012.

———. *The Trinity*. Translated by Stephen McKenna. Edited by Roy J. Deferrari. FOTC 25. 1954.

Jerome. *Commentary on Galatians*. Translated by Andrew Cain. Edited by David G. Hunter. FOTC 121. 2010.

———. *Commentary on Matthew*. Translated by Thomas P. Scheck. Edited by Thomas P. Halton. FOTC 117. 2008.

———. *Dogmatic and Polemical Works*. Translated by John N. Hritzu. Edited by Hermigild Dressler. FOTC 53. 1965.

———. *The Homilies of Saint Jerome (1–59 on the Psalms)*. Vol. 1. Translated by Marie Liguori Ewald. Edited by Hermigild Dressler. FOTC 48. 1964.

———. *The Homilies of Saint Jerome (Homilies 60–96)*. Vol. 2. Translated by Marie Liguori Ewald. Edited by Roy J. Deferrari. FOTC 57. 1966.

———. *On Illustrious Men*. Edited and translated by Thomas P. Halton. FOTC 100. 1999.

John Chrysostom. *Apologist*. Translated by Margaret A. Schatkin and Paul W. Harkins. Edited by Thomas P. Halton. FOTC 73. 1985.

———. *Commentary on Saint John the Apostle and Evangelist: Homilies 1–47*. Translated by Thomas Aquinas Goggin. FOTC 33. 1957.

———. *Commentary on Saint John the Apostle and Evangelist: Homilies 48–88*. Translated by Thomas Aquinas Goggin. FOTC 41. 1959.

———. *Discourses against Judaizing Christians*. Translated by Paul W. Harkins. FOTC 68. 1979.

———. *Homilies on Genesis 1–17*. Translated by Robert C. Hill. Edited by Thomas P. Halton. FOTC 74. 1986.

———. *Homilies on Genesis 18–45*. Translated by Robert C. Hill. Edited by Thomas P. Halton. FOTC 82. 1990.

———. *Homilies on Genesis 46–67*. Translated by Robert C. Hill. Edited by Thomas P. Halton. FOTC 87. 1992.

————. *On the Incomprehensible Nature of God.* Translated by Paul W. Harkins. Edited by Hermigild Dressler. FOTC 72. 1984.

————. *On Repentance and Almsgiving.* Translated by Gus George Christo. Edited by Thomas P. Halton. FOTC 96. 1998.

————. *On Wealth and Poverty.* Translated by Catharine P. Roth. Popular Patristics Series 9. Crestwood, N.Y.: St Vladimir's Seminary Press, 1981.

John Damascene. *Writings.* Translated by Frederic H. Chase, Jr. Edited by Hermigild Dressler. FOTC 37. 1958.

Justin Martyr. *The First Apology, The Second Apology, Dialogue with Trypho, Exhortation to the Greeks, Discourse to the Greeks, The Monarchy or The Rule of God.* Translated by Thomas B. Falls. FOTC 6. 1948.

Lactantius. *The Divine Institutes, Books I–VII.* Translated by Mary Francis McDonald. Edited by Roy J. Deferrari. FOTC 49. 1964.

————. *The Minor Works.* Translated by Mary Francis McDonald. Edited by Roy J. Deferrari. FOTC 54. 1965.

Leo the Great. *Letters.* Translated by Edmund Hunt. Edited by Roy J. Deferrari. FOTC 34. 1957.

————. *Sermons.* Translated by Jane Patricia Freeland and Agnes Josephine Conway. Edited by Thomas P. Halton. FOTC 93. 1996.

Marius Victorinus. *Theological Treatises on the Trinity.* Translated by Mary T. Clark. Edited by Hermigild Dressler. FOTC 69. 1981.

Martin of Braga, Paschasius of Dumium, and Leander of Seville. *Iberian Fathers.* Vol. 1. Translated by Claude W. Barlow. FOTC 62. 1969.

Niceta of Remesiana, Sulpicius Severus, Vincent of Lerins, Prosper of Aquitaine. *Writings; Commonitories; Grace and Free Will.* Translated by Rudolph E. Morris. Edited by Bernard M. Peebles. FOTC 7. 1949.

Novatian. *The Trinity, The Spectacles, Jewish Foods, In Praise of Purity, Letters.* Translated by Russell J. DeSimone. Edited by Hermigild Dressler. FOTC 67. 1974.

Oecumenius. *Commentary on the Apocalypse.* Translated by John N. Suggit. FOTC 112. 2006.

Origen. *Commentary on the Epistle to the Romans, Books 1–5.* Translated by Thomas P. Scheck. Edited by Thomas P. Halton. FOTC 103. 2001.

————. *Commentary on the Epistle to the Romans, Books 6–10.* Translated by Thomas P. Scheck. Edited by Thomas P. Halton. FOTC 104. 2002.

————. *Commentary on the Gospel according to John, Books 1–10.* Translated by Ronald E. Heine. FOTC 80. 1989.

————. *Commentary on the Gospel according to John, Books 13–32.* Translated by Ronald E. Heine. Edited by Thomas P. Halton. FOTC 89. 1993.

————. *Homilies on Genesis and Exodus.* Translated by Ronald E. Heine. Edited by Hermigild Dressler. FOTC 71. 1982.

————. *Homilies on Jeremiah and Homily on 1 Kings 28.* Translated by John Clark Smith. Edited by Thomas P. Halton. FOTC 97. 1998.

————. *Homilies on Joshua.* Translated by Barbara J. Bruce. Edited by Thomas P. Halton and Cynthia White. FOTC 105. 2002.

———. *Homilies on Judges.* Translated by Elizabeth Ann Dively Lauro. Edited by Thomas P. Halton. FOTC 119. 2010.

———. *Homilies on Leviticus 1–16.* Translated by Gary Wayne Barkley. Edited by Thomas P. Halton. FOTC 83. 1990.

———. *Homilies on Luke and Fragments on Luke.* Translated by Joseph T. Lienhard. Edited by Thomas P. Halton. FOTC 94. 2009.

Orosius of Braga. *The Seven Books of History against the Pagans.* Translated by Roy J. Deferrari. Edited by Hermigild Dressler. FOTC 50. 1964.

Pacian of Barcelona and Orosius of Braga. *Iberian Fathers.* Vol. 3. Translated by Craig L. Hanson. Edited by Thomas P. Halton. FOTC 99. 1999.

Pamphilus of Caesarea. *Apology for Origen: With the Letter of Rufinus on the Falsification of the Books of Origen.* Translated by Thomas P. Scheck. FOTC 120. 2010.

Peter Chrysologus and Valerian. *Selected Sermons of Saint Peter Chrysologus and Saint Valerian's Homilies.* Translated by George E. Ganss. Edited by Hermigild Dressler. FOTC 17. 1953.

Peter Chrysologus. *Selected Sermons of Saint Peter Chrysologus.* Translated by William B. Palardy. Edited by Thomas P. Halton. FOTC 109. 2004.

———. *Selected Sermons of Saint Peter Chrysologus.* Translated by William B. Palardy. Edited by Thomas P. Halton. FOTC 110. 2005.

Pontius, Paulinus, Possidius, Athanasius, Jerome, Ennodius, and Hilary. *Early Christian Biographies.* Translated by Roy J. Deferrari, John A. Lacy, Mary Magdeleine Müller, Mary Emily Keenan, Marie Liguori Ewald, and Genevieve Marie Cook. Edited by Hermigild Dressler and Roy J. Deferrari. FOTC 15. 1952.

Prudentius. *The Poems of Prudentius.* Vol. 1. Translated by M. Clement Eagan. Edited by Hermigild Dressler. FOTC 43. 1962.

———. *The Poems of Prudentius.* Vol. 2. Translated by M. Clement Eagan. Edited by Roy J. Deferrari. FOTC 52. 1965.

Salvian. *The Writings of Salvian, the Presbyter.* Translated by Jeremiah F. O'Sullivan. Edited by Ludwig Schopp. FOTC 3. 1947.

Tertullian and Minucius Felix. *Apologetical Works and Octavius.* Translated by Rudolph Arbesmann, Emily Joseph Daly, and Edwin A. Quain. Edited by Roy J. Deferrari. FOTC 10. 1950.

Tertullian. *Disciplinary, Moral, and Ascetical Works.* Translated by Rudolph Arbesmann, Emily Joseph Daly, and Edwin A. Quain. Edited by Hermigild Dressler. FOTC 40. 1959.

Theodore of Mopsuestia. *Commentary on the Twelve Prophets.* Translated by Robert C. Hill. Edited by Thomas P. Halton. FOTC 108. 2004.

Theodoret of Cyrus. *Commentary on the Psalms 1–72.* Translated by Robert C. Hill. FOTC 101. 2000.

———. *Commentary on the Psalms: Psalms 73–150.* Translated by Robert C. Hill. Edited by Thomas P. Halton. FOTC 102. 2001.

———. *Eranistes.* Translated by Gerard H. Ettlinger. FOTC 106. 2003.

INDEX OF FATHERS

References are to quote numbers.

SUBJECT INDEX

References are to quote numbers.

Other books in the *Sayings of the Fathers of the Church* series

The Seven Deadly Sins
Edited by Kevin M. Clarke
Foreword by Mike Aquilina

Also from The Catholic University of America Press

The Light of Christ: An Introduction to Catholicism
Thomas Joseph White, OP

The Intellectual Life: Its Spirit, Conditions, and Method
A. G. Sertillanges, OP
Foreword by James V. Schall

Ossa Latinitatis Sola: Ad Mentem Reginaldi Rationemque
Reginaldus Thomas Foster and Daniel Patricius McCarthy

Augustine in His Own Words
Edited by William Harmless, SJ

The Quotable Augustine
Saint Augustine
Foreword by James V. Schall

The Vision of the Soul: Truth, Goodness, and Beauty in the Western Tradition
James Matthew Wilson

Called to Holiness: On Love, Vocation, and Formation
Pope Emeritus Benedict XVI
Edited by Pietro Rossotti

Renewing the Mind: A Reader in the Philosophy of Catholic Education
Ryan N. S. Topping

Death, Judgment, Heaven & Hell was designed in Scala with Hypatia Sans and Scala Sans display type and composed by Kachergis Book Design of Pittsboro, North Carolina. It was printed on 60-pound Natural Eggshell and bound by McNaughton & Gunn of Saline, Michigan.